The
Flower
Arranger's
A-Z

The Flower Arranger's A-Z

Daphne Vagg

B. T. Batsford Ltd.

To the memory of Jean Taylor, teacher and friend, who gave inspiration to so many flower arrangers.

ISBN 0 7134 6835 1

Typeset by Servis Filmsetting Ltd, Manchester
and printed in Great Britain by
The Bath Press, Bath

for the publishers
B. T. Batsford Ltd
583 Fulham Road
London SW6 5BY

PREFACE

The Flower Arranger's A–Z is intended to fill a gap in the now substantial literature on flower arrangement, and to provide a handy-sized, alphabetical, ready reference book for all arrangers – beginners and experienced, students and teachers, show competitors, church rota arrangers and the 'flowers-in-the-home' enthusiasts.

Something more than dictionary definitions was needed, so, within the limits of the space allowed, I have included as much information as possible, with observations from my own experience in flower arranging.

It was tempting to try to include more about plants, the arranger's medium, but far more detail than I would have had space for is readily available in a host of gardening and wild flower reference books.

Acknowledgements

I acknowledge most gratefully my debt to: arrangers, past and present, here and abroad, who have generously shared their knowledge and experience; those who lent photographs of their arrangements for use in this book; NAFAS, for its unfailing support; Bettye, who typed all the manuscript with industry and enthusiasm; and above all, my husband, John, for the drawings, the colour photographs and many of the black and white ones. No reader will need me to point out the inestimable value of his contribution to the book.

Daphne Vagg

Except where otherwise acknowledged, the arrangements are by the author.

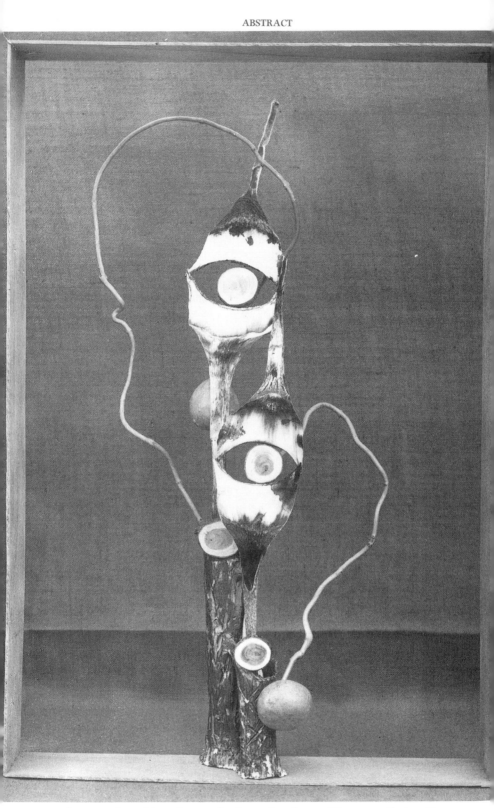

Abstract *A striking abstract by Betty Booth at a Harrogate Spring Show.*

ABSTRACT

If only the word 'abstract' began with a letter 'Z' it could be at the end of the book, where it would be more suitable, because it is usually the last style that an arranger comes to. Abstract flower arrangement makes sense only if one is prepared to accept that flower arranging is an art form and that arrangers, like artists and sculptors, may experiment with and explore their medium – that is, plant material. Abstract work is far removed from the naturalistic arranging of pretty flowers and attractive foliages; instead plant material is treated as textured and coloured geometric units in a carefully thought out design. A rose is used because it is a velvety circular shape; an onion seedhead is a rough-textured sphere; arum leaves are green triangles; and gladioli are spikes of scarlet colour.

Abstraction, as a concept, is neither new nor divorced from everyday life. Meaning 'to extract', 'to summarize', 'to represent the essence and strip away non-essentials' or 'the ideal or theoretical way of regarding things', abstraction or simplification has been used in many ways throughout the centuries. The cave paintings at Lascaux depicted animals with a few strokes; fifteenth-century Japanese sand and rock gardens eliminated plants; Picasso showed images from different viewpoints all in one painting; firms and organizations are recognized by their trademarks; road signs warn or instruct with simple lines and shapes; and the caricaturist exaggerates features to typify a person. We accept and understand this visual shorthand.

The advent of the camera in the latter part of the nineteenth century released artists from the need to record details of scenes and events. They were then able to explore new ways of treating their subject matter and of putting paint onto canvas, and the Impressionists led the way to Fauvism, Cubism, Surrealism, Pop and Op art. Sculpture and architecture followed similar lines seeking to show 'the inner geometry'.

Experiments in abstract flower arranging began in the 1960s, influenced by the general artistic and design scene, the restraint of **ikebana** (q.v.) and the mood of the decade to 'do one's own thing'. In the UK, arrangers were influenced by the work and books of American arrangers such as Emma Hodgkinson Cyphers, Dorothy Reister, Francis Bode and Helen van Pelt Wilson.

For the next 20 years there was a good deal of discussion and disagreement about whether an abstract flower design was truly abstract *or* merely **free-style** (q.v.) (free-form, free-line, free-expression, modern or contemporary – call it what you will); and whether it was decorative (non-objective and just a pattern) *or* expressive (objective, interpretative, with a meaning). By the late 1980s Britain had settled for 'modern/abstract' as a description in competitive shows, for, in truth, no hard and fast dividing line had ever been possible. With hindsight, no-one should have tried to pin down a style that was essentially exploratory and experimental. Even the word 'style' is perhaps a misnomer, yet, over the years certain characteristics have been observed and have come to be accepted as yardsticks (often too rigidly applied) for assessing and judging abstract designs in flower arrangement. Just as artists and sculptors tried to get as far away as possible from traditional styles so the flower arranger tried to get away from traditional massed design by stressing all the opposites. Beauty is seen not as chocolate-box prettiness, but in the 'bones' of the design.

Characteristics
No design is likely to show all these qualities, but an effective abstract will certainly show some.

1 Plant material is not used naturalistically, but chosen for its design attributes.
2 The design is pared down to essentials and each item plays a definite part.
3 The traditional focal area may not be evident; there may be points of interest all over the design.
4 The container, if visible, will be a unit in the overall design, not just a holder of water and mechanics.
5 Accessories, if any, are in themselves abstract, such as 'found objects', industrial waste or nature's own abstracts – weathered wood and flints.
6 Plant material may be altered and manipulated: painted (most overseas arrangers think that British arrangers paint too much), looped, sliced, bent, twisted, stripped.
7 Bases and backing are used as integral parts to create depth and interest.
8 Asymmetry is more likely than symmetry.

Problems for arrangers
Keen gardeners and arrangers whose work is, or has been, strongly traditional and naturalistic often find abstract flower arranging a difficult concept. Even today, comparatively few of us have homes and furnishings for which it is suitable, and devising suitable containers, mechanics and supports can cause problems. The approach to it, also, has to be more intellectual than spontaneous, but the rewards are many. The creative arranger sees abstract as a challenge to create new forms of beauty, and as a boundless opportunity to explore new ideas either for decoration or as a means of self-expression. For the arrangers who are prepared to attempt abstract work, even just as an exercise and a discipline, the *very least* that will be gained is an awareness of the value of space, form and texture and the pleasure that goes with it. Their traditional work will improve astonishingly from this new perspective. At best, abstract opens doors and windows that arrangers have not even glimpsed before, linking their art with exciting developments in other arts and crafts.

ACCESSORY
In competitive work an accessory is an item of non-plant material included in, or grouped with, a flower arrangement exhibit. Containers, mechanics, bases, drapes, backgrounds and exhibit titles are not usually included in the term, but competition rules do vary, so it is wise to check, especially if exhibiting in another country. Stones, candles, figurines, feathers, pottery, glass, metal and shells are some of the most popular items but virtually anything may count as an accessory, including, under NAFAS rules, items of plant material which have been tooled or crafted to become something different, e.g., a bird's nest, corn dolly or wooden figurine.

Accessories can:

- help the interpretation of a title or theme
- provide extra interest when flowers are few or expensive
- be a source of inspiration for an arrangement, suggested by line, colour, pattern or association

Some accessories, like candles, feathers or stones, may be used as part of, or within, the arrangement; others, like a figurine or an ornament, may be used beside the flowers, and it then helps to have a base to unify the two. In show work the accessory must not predominate over the plant material, and there should always be a link between the two of colour, line, shape or perhaps association.

Scale is always important. Accessories, especially figurines, birds or animals that are too small can look finicky and ridiculous; if too large, they dominate and dwarf the plant material. When several accessories are being used with one arrangement, they must be in scale with each other: a large bird with a small horse can ruin the illusion of a landscape design, and, less obviously, a toy yacht, with a full-size pennant nearby, can look equally at odds. Putting a large accessory farther back in the exhibit makes it seem smaller, and one that is rather too small can be made to look more important if raised up on a small base.

It is a sound idea to begin arranging with the accessory in place, then there is no chance that it will look like an afterthought. Several small accessories are usually better if they are grouped together instead of being dotted about the design.

In the home, and in church, the position is reversed and it is the flower arrangements that become the 'accessories' to the interior decor, furnishings and architecture. But the considerations of suitability and overall harmony still hold good, and to be effective there must be positive links between the two. (*See* FIGURINE, STILL LIFE **and colour section**)

ADAM, ROBERT (1728–92)

Architect-interior designer in the neo-classical style who employed other famous eighteenth-century craftsmen to carry out his work. Examples may be seen at Syon House and Osterley Park near London, Harewood House, Yorkshire and Kedleston Hall, Derbyshire.

Of special interest to, and inspiration for, the arranger are Adam's elegant swags and garlands of flowers, leaves and fruit, usually painted white or gilded, on walls and ceilings of turquoise, pale blue, grey-green and rose-pink.

ADDITIVES TO WATER

In an attempt to prolong the vase-life of cut flowers and foliage, various substances have, from time to time, been added to water, e.g., sugar, gin, vinegar, copper coins, mild disinfectant, mild household bleach, washing-up liquid, aspirin, fizzy lemonade and proprietary compounds such as Chrysal. Opinions vary as to their effectiveness, and scientific evidence is scarce, except that it is known that a mild solution of aspirin closes the stomata of green leaves and stems and so reduces water loss. (Try half a soluble aspirin tablet to a pint of water.)

Commercial additives for vase water usually contain sugar, a bactericide and an acidifying agent. Try making a home-brew from $\frac{1}{2}$ pint water, $\frac{1}{2}$ tablespoon sugar and $\frac{1}{2}$ teaspoon of bleach. (*See* CONDITIONING)

ADHESIVES

The range today is extensive and varied. Choose from these examples; follow the maker's instructions.

Type	Product
For fabric, hessian	Copydex, UHU, Bostik and Loctite Clear
For paper, cardboard	Polycell/Solvite wallpaper pastes for large areas; Gloy paste/gum, Gripfix paste. Stephen's Golden Gum, UHU Stic, Pritt stick
General purpose – sticks metal, ceramics, wood, leather, cork, glass and many plastics	UHU, Bostik and Loctite Clear, Dunlop Thixofix
For vinyl	Loctite Vinyl mender
Superglues for mending containers, general tough repairs	Bostik Superglue Gel, Araldite, Loctite Super Glue, UHU Supalok
Heavy duty putty-like strip for securing pinholders, metal, glass, plastics, ceramics	Oasis-fix
Re-usable mastic for charts/pictures to walls, etc.	Blue-tack, Plant-tack, Pritt-tak, Sellotape Sticky Fixing Strip
Glue sticks and pens	UHU Gluepen (for paper), Tack A Note (removable and reusable), Fastik
For collage	UHU, Bostik Clear, Gloy Children's Glue (non-stringing)
For découpage	Bath/kitchen silicone sealant, e.g., Sealastic, Aquaria
For children (non-toxic)	Gloy Children's Glue, Pritt Stick, UHU Gluepen (sponge-tipped), Marvin Medium
Glue guns (expensive but fast acting and clean to use; electric point needed)	Bostik TG4 with hot-melt stick refills
Spray can (fast-drying, water resistant for plant material, paper, foil, plastic film, Styrofoam, felts)	3M Floral Adhesive

AFTER CARE

Fresh arrangements: place out of direct sunlight and draughts and away from fires and radiators. Top up the water daily (twice in the first 24 hours) and, if possible, mist-spray daily to maintain humidity and reduce water loss. Protect polished surfaces as you do this (*See* TOPPING UP).

Dried and preserved arrangements: strong light or sunlight will fade colours, though this may be desired for glycerined leaves. When dusty, or if mildew develops, swish glycerined leaves through soapy water, rinse, and dry thoroughly if they are to be packed away. Glycerined material is best stored in boxes or paper bags, rather than polythene, which encourages sweating. Refresh flattened and crushed preserved materials by holding them in the steam of a boiling kettle and gently reshaping with gloved hands. Frequent blowing or gentle brushing with a soft-haired paint brush will keep dried arrangements looking clean and cared for. When the dust gets too thick it is time to take the arrangement apart, clean the pieces and start again!

AIR DRYING, *see* DRYING

AIR PLANTS

Plants of the genus *Tillandsia*, in the Bromeliad family, grow without soil of any kind, absorbing moisture from the air. Originating in Central and South America, they became popular in Britain in the 1980s. Fix them with a spot or two of adhesive to any surface, such as driftwood, bark, slate, marble, shell or tile and mist-spray lightly once a day or so.

AMERICAN COLONIAL (1620–1800)

This period is of unique interest in that it shows how European culture and customs were adapted to a new country with different climate, plants and problems. It also marks the beginning of dried and preserved plants being used for decorative, rather than just culinary and medicinal, purposes. The life of the first settlers in America was hard and a struggle for survival. What they could not grow or make had to be imported from Europe on an arduous four-month voyage. Nevertheless, by the end of the seventeenth century, the colonies on the eastern seaboard were thriving, and the eighteenth century saw an increase in wealth, craftsmen's skills and living standards.

The restored part of colonial Williamsburg, Virginia, America, has come to be synonymous with American colonial living of the late seventeenth and eighteenth centuries, and it has many affinities with Georgian England.

Gardens, at first, had to be cultivated in virgin soil and protected from invaders. Initially, they were cultivated solely for food and medicinal herbs, but later flower and leisure gardens were developed.

Settings
The early settlers had very basic homes with exposed timbers, earth-packed floors, shutters rather than glass windows, simple utensils, homespun fabric, patchwork and rush-lights. The 'keeping' room, as it was called, served as the family's living room and kitchen and often bedroom as well.

By the early eighteenth century homes had become much more elegant with painted and stencilled, or pine- and cedar-panelled, walls; Queen Anne and, later, Georgian furniture; china imported from Holland, Germany and Britain; and finer fabrics.

Colours
No special ones are significant, but in the seventeenth century dyes would have been produced from plants, and colours were therefore subtle and muted. Later, fine silks and cottons were imported.

Plant materials
Seventeenth-century arrangements comprised herbs, wild flowers and fruits picked for medicinal and culinary use.

Eighteenth-century flowers were far more varied and were grown for pleasure and cutting. Golden rod (solidago), black-eyed Susan (rudbeckia), maple, dogwood, scarlet oak, hickory, cocks' comb and Indian (sweet) corn were indigenous plants added to those seeds and bulbs brought or sent over from Europe. Old favourites included rose, poppy, wallflower, tulip, stock, hollyhock, marigold, monkshood and ox-eye daisies.

Flowers for drying included strawflowers (helichrysum), pearly ever-lastings (anaphalis), globe amaranth (gomphrena), globe thistle (echinops), honesty (lunaria), sea lavender (limonium) and statice.

Containers
At first, simple utensils, sturdily made of iron, pewter, wood or earthenware were used. Later Chinese export bowls and vases, Delft or English blue and white flower bricks and urns, porcelain from England or Germany, and salt glaze vases were added to the range.

Arrangements
Based on a study of eighteenth-century prints, books and fabrics, Williams-burg has revived fan-shaped, massed arrangements of mixed flowers and leaves for fresh summer and dried winter arrangements. Fruit and foliage groups decorate tables, and at Christmas time, evergreen garlands made of yew, holly, box, pine, fir, ivy, rosemary and bayberry are used with apples, lemons, oranges and fircones. The exteriors are garlanded with mountain laurel and white pine. (*See* **PERIOD ARRANGING**)

ANNIVERSARIES
If called on to provide flowers for an anniversary or jubilee, the arranger can, with some thought, use more than just the appropriate colour. For example

drift-wood and branches for the wooden anniversary; the silvery seed-cases of honesty (*Lunaria annua*) for 'pearl'; tough glycerined leaves for 'leather'; and gypsophila or Queen Anne's lace (*Anthriscus sylvestris*) for 'lace'. The best known symbolic anniversaries are:

1st	paper	9th	pottery or willow	25th	silver
2nd	cotton	10th	tin	30th	pearl
3rd	leather	11th	steel	35th	coral
4th	fruit and flowers	12th	silk or linen	40th	ruby
5th	wooden	13th	lace	45th	sapphire
6th	sugar or iron	14th	ivory	50th	golden
7th	wool or copper	15th	crystal	55th	emerald
8th	bronze or pottery	20th	china	60th	diamond

ART DECO (1920–39)

Where **Art Nouveau** (q.v.) took much of its inspiration from curving natural plant forms and was crowded and complex, Art Deco broke away to the abstract clarity of straight lines and geometric shapes with areas of colour for colour's sake, taking features from Egyptian, African, Mexican and Central American art. The name was taken (later) from the Paris exhibition of *Arts Décoratifs* in 1925. The style, like Art Nouveau, affected architecture (particularly cinemas and factories of the 1930s), furniture, china, ornaments and posters. It was typified by glossy surfaces like chrome, mirrors and black glass; frosted glass; enamelled finishes; Bakelite; Clarice Cliff pottery; and sun-ray patterns for wireless sets and radiator grilles.

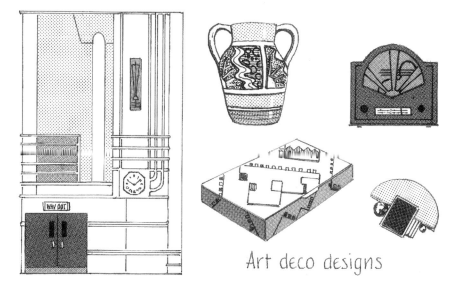

Art deco designs

No flower arrangement style developed in the 1920s and '30s in keeping with Art Deco. Its geometric lines were too far removed from the naturalistic style of flower arrangement at the time. Flowers would, even so, have been arranged in vases and bowls shaped and decorated with Art Deco motifs. Some of the modern/abstract work of the 1970s, however, shows characteristics more akin to the geometry of Art Deco. (*See* **NINETEEN TWENTIES AND THIRTIES** and **PERIOD ARRANGING**)

ART NOUVEAU (1890–1910)

The decorative style known as Art Nouveau (the 'new art') swept through Europe and America at the end of the nineteenth century. It had its origins in William Morris's Arts and Crafts movement and owed its asymmetry to Rococo and Japanese influences. The style is typified by sinuous, curving plant forms and whiplash stems, flowing draperies and willowy female forms. The style affected architecture and interior decor, furniture, ornaments, lamp shades, dress, jewellery and glass.

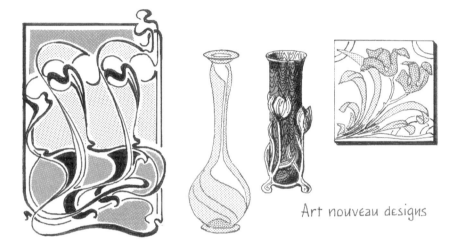

Art nouveau designs

Plant forms most commonly seen in Art Nouveau designs include the acanthus leaf, bluebell, convolvulus, honesty (*Lunaria annua*) seedhead, honeysuckle, iris, lily, lily-of-the-valley, nasturtium, poppy and its seedhead, teasel, violet and water-lily.

There cannot truly be said to be an Art Nouveau style of arranging, though undoubtedly the movement encouraged a simpler, more naturalistic approach. A present day design can attempt to interpret the specific artistic style using the plants mentioned above, but not easily! (*See* **EDWARDIAN** and **PERIOD ARRANGING**)

ARTIFICIAL FLOWERS

The acceptability of artificial flowers (whether made from fabric, paper, feathers, shells or any other material) in arrangements is controversial. There are those who contend that flower arrangements should be completely natural, even though some materials may be dried, preserved with glycerine, painted or dyed.

In recent years the glut of good quality polyester and silk flowers, mainly from the Orient, has meant that many a florist's shop or flower club sales' table is more than half-filled with artificial flowers and foliage. Much of it is so good a reproduction that you have to look at it carefully to discover whether it is real or fake. This, in turn, has led to large artificial displays in shops, offices, hotels and public buildings where central heating shortens

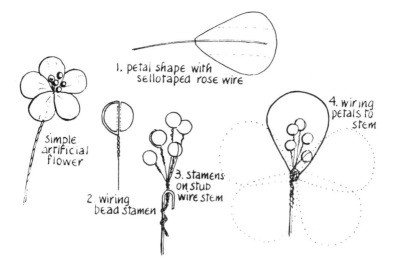

1. petal shape with sellotaped rose wire

simple artificial flower

2. wiring bead stamen

3. stamens on stub wire stem

4. wiring petals to stem

Artificial Flowers *Making a simple artificial flower from paper, fabric or ribbon. Use this as a basic method to devise different centres and petals, and made flowers of graded sizes into a spray.*

the life of fresh flowers, and also in homes in winter. The initial outlay is high, but the flowers and leaves can be maintained easily and last for years.

Artificial flowers have a long and distinguished history, not only for decorating millinery and dress. For centuries the Chinese have made their beautiful paper flowers from the pith of a reed plant; the Greeks and Etruscans made wreaths and chaplets of oak and ivy leaves out of gold; eighteenth-century Meissen and present day Royal Worcester porcelain flowers still delight us; and the exquisite gold and jewelled flowers of Carl Fabergé are supreme works of art.

The Victorians produced flowers in all manner of materials such as beads, wool, shells and hair, and in this century the craft of making flowers from barbola paste and 'Glitterwax', huge Mexican 'fun' flowers from crêpe paper and roses from ribbon or nylon tights has given pleasure to many.

It was probably the cheap plastic flowers given away with detergent packets in the 1960s that prejudiced so many people against the use of imitations in flower arrangement. For the most part artificial plant material is still not permitted in competitive show work, except perhaps at Christmas, and then only if the schedule specifically says so. Artificial flowers should not be confused with what have come to be called **made-up flowers** (q.v.). These are made predominantly from dried or preserved natural plant material – with any necessary addition of wires, tape and glue – and are permitted at most shows. A further distinction is often made between commercially produced and hand-made flowers. At Christmas time arrangers like to make their own flowers of foil, crêpe or flocked paper or ribbon, often using baubles or beads as stamens. The result is flower-like but not usually intended to be an accurate copy. One of the simplest methods of making a flower from inexpensive waterproof florists' ribbon is shown in the above diagram. The number, size and shape of the petals can be varied. Petals made from crêpe papers do not usually need wiring as the paper can be stretched and curled as needed.

BACKGROUNDS

The use of a background behind a flower arrangement is mostly confined to show or exhibition/display work, where it can:

- help to focus attention
- create the illusion of depth
- enhance the exhibit with a chosen colour
- add to the atmosphere or mood
- suggest a period-style setting
- provide support/water supply for plant material, expecially for a modern/abstract

In shows it is important that a background does not overwhelm the arrangement. Avoid too strong or bright a colour; shiny, light-catching surfaces (take care with mirrors, polished metals, satin-finish, patterned or lurex fabrics); painted scenes that are too bold and detailed; and eye-catching lettering on a poster, newspaper, etc. Generally it is safer to provide a backing of greyed tones or muted colourings with a matt surface, and if painted, with only the merest suggestion of clouds and trees or the outline of buildings or interior decor. As a golden rule, understatement pays off.

Triangular-draped fabrics, so popular in the 1960s and early '70s, gave way to a more tailored use of fabric, covering panels or the whole of the background or niche, and in the mid-70s painted scenic backgrounds were very popular. Exhibitors soon learned that it was far more effective merely to suggest a scene or to use gently mottled abstract backings. Shaping the backboard with rounded corners at the top or echoing arches or other architectural shapes can add much to an exhibit. For abstract exhibits, you can use the background to increase depth by fixing part of the design to it and, if necessary, to conceal a water supply.

The support of any background, and especially one that has to take weight or hide a container, presents some problems on a show bench, which is

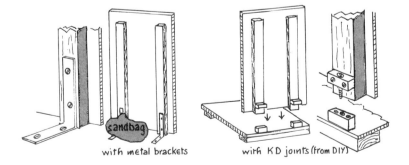

with metal brackets   with KD joints (from DIY)

Backgrounds *Two ways of supporting backgrounds.*

normally comparatively narrow from front to back. An effective method is to combine the backboard with a base using KD joints (from hardware shops), or to use brackets as feet at the back, with bricks or weights on them for stability.

Backgrounds are usually made from hardboard, chipboard, plywood, softboard or thick cardboard strengthened with glued-on wooden battens, but they can be of any material to suit the exhibit. Emulsion paints are available in a huge range of colours, and spray paints can be used for a variety of effects. The decorative possibilities are endless, and it is tempting to make the background a work of art in itself. Keep in mind at all times that it *is* a background and is there solely to enhance the flower arrangement.

Exhibitors should always check with the schedule that a background is permitted and for the size of the space allowed. Make the backing *smaller* than this to allow for inaccurate staging, especially at shows in a marquee where the ground may be uneven. (*See* **DRAPE**)

BALANCE

Balance is an important **design principle** (q.v.). Our sense of balance is one of stability achieved by uprights which are absolutely vertical and horizontals crossing them at right angles. If anything leans over too far from the vertical it actually falls over because of the pull of gravity, unless some weight or counter-balance holds it steady. Our inherent awareness of actual and visual balance means that we are ill at ease when something lacks these qualities. Balance is therefore very important in flower arrangements.

Symmetry
This is the easiest balance to appreciate and to achieve, hence the popularity of the symmetrical, triangular arrangement. Everything on one side of an imaginary central vertical line is balanced by something of similar size and colour, and within the same area, on the other. Both 'halves' need not be absolutely identical, and one large pink flower on the right may be balanced by two smaller ones on the left, but they will be equal visually. A long slender spray on one side may be balanced by a shorter, thicker one on the other, or a pale pink rose by a cream carnation of much the same size. But the pale rose would not be balanced by a dark red carnation because the colours have different weights, and the arrangement would look unbalanced.

Asymmetry
Asymmetrical balance is more difficult to achieve, but is usually far more interesting. The two vertical 'halves' of a design or arrangement are not similar in outline or content. Bolder, more densely grouped features on one side are balanced by a larger area of smaller items *and more space* on the other. Larger leaves on the left may be balanced by long-stemmed branches or blossom on the right, or three small buds on the left by one larger flower on the right. In a landscape design the branch representing a tree with flowers and leaves beneath, is often balanced by an expanse of water, some stones and one or two smaller leaves.

Top- and bottom-heaviness
It is easy to recognize top-heaviness because anything large at the top and small at the bottom is bound to respond to gravity and topple over. Bottom-heaviness is less easy to recognize because it gives a secure, stable feeling.

But elegance, good proportions and rhythm are often lost in a flower arrangement by clumsy bottom-heaviness caused by too large or too thick a container or base.

BASES

Although a base is usually defined as anything on which a flower container stands, in flower arrangements it is part of the whole design and not just an afterthought to protect the furniture, though obviously it serves that purpose as well.

A base can unify a group of arrangements or an arrangement and accessories; add colour and texture to an arrangement; and help to emphasize the interpretation.

It is important that the shape, colour, texture and material of the base should be in keeping with the style of the exhibit, for example, a slice of wood, slate or stone for a naturalistic landscape; perspex triangles or rectangles for a modern angular design; a velvet-covered, braid-trimmed drum for a classical cupid container; or a tailored hessian-covered shape for hand-thrown pottery. Colours are always safer if they are greyed and toned down, and very shiny surfaces (mirrors or polished metal) should be used with care so that they are not eye-catching.

A base with feet, or raised up by a wood block or tin glued to the underside, gives an area of shadow beneath the design and this increases the sense of space.

With an asymmetrical design, angle the base across the space available to give more interest and greater depth.

Don't overdo the base; in show work bases are often too large or piled on top of each other, making an exhibit bottom-heavy. This is particularly common in landscape designs where wood and stone are piled up to provide a woodland base, quite out of proportion to the slender branch, making the 'tree' above. Tall vertical containers with sleek modern designs are often seen on oval bases which introduce a horizontal line quite out of keeping with the line of the arrangement.

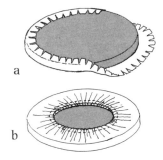

Bases *Two ways of covering a round or oval base:*
(a) fabric cut ready for gluing to the underside;
(b) an elasticated, removable mob-cap.

Most arrangers like to have several fabric 'mob-cap' covers for round or oval bases so that they can ring the colour changes. Brushed nylon, or any fabric with a little stretch to it, is ideal for this.

Cut out a shape 6 or 7 cm (2½ in.) larger all round than the base, which can be a silver cake-board or similar. Machine, or hand-stitch a narrow hem and thread round elastic through it. Knot the elastic and stretch the mob-cap over the base, smoothing into a neatly tailored fit.

If you prefer a permanent cover, cut the fabric 2 cm (¾ in.) larger all round; cut notches half that extra width all round and glue to the underside of the board, stretching the fabric tightly over the front of the board as you do so. This produces a perfectly tailored base which can be decorated with braid or cord.

BASKETS

Baskets are usually made from plaited or woven natural plant materials: cane, rush, osier (willow), rattan, palm, bamboo, raffia or other pliable branches and roots, according to their country of origin, so they have a natural affinity with flowers, foliage and fruit and have been used over the centuries, in almost every civilization, as receptacles for gathering, storing, displaying and serving. Many are left in their natural state; some are stained

and varnished. There are, of course, basket shapes made in other, non-woven materials such as ceramics, glass and metal, which can make attractive flower containers, but they are not usually acceptable when a basket is asked for in competitive work.

Shapes and styles vary considerably, from the sturdy, peasant types to the sophisticated presentation basket, gilded and high-handled. It is important to suit the style of arrangement and type of plant material to the basket container. Loosely arranged garden or wild flowers, leaves and foliage suit a simple country basket, while hot-house and exotic flowers look more appropriate in a lighter, daintier shape. In the 1960s a strong diagonal line was popular for arrangements in baskets and boxes, but today it looks contrived. Asymmetry, however, is interesting where there is a lid or handle. If the basket has a handle, most of it should be allowed to show or there is no point in choosing it as a container. A lidded basket is most effective propped partly open and the lid partly shown, though the flowers should not look squashed in. Such an arrangement is very economical of flowers and foliage because 'the back' will not be seen. Flat or almost flat basketry makes a useful base for display.

Present day arrangers place an unobtrusive plastic box, tin or glass/ceramic bowl inside the basket to hold the mechanics and water for a fresh arrangement. If the basket sides are too deep for ease of arranging, a block or inverted tin under the container solves that problem.

Show organizers should remember that a basket is not easily staged in a tall niche, for the competitor is then almost certainly forced to raise the basket on some block or stand to fill the space allotted. They then run the risk of having a bare-looking exhibit, or one with plant material so tall that it is out of proportion to the basket container. Open tabling is better.
(*See* CONTAINERS)

BEST IN/ON SHOW

Ideally, this accolade should be exactly what it implies: an award for the best exhibit of all the first prize-winners. But, increasingly, classes are being excluded and considered ineligible and the award is in danger of being devalued. Many shows exclude group entries from consideration for the award and the so-called 'craft classes' such as collages, pressed flower pictures, and mobiles which are brought ready-made for final staging at a show. The argument against the latter is that they can be prepared at leisure and improved for several months beforehand and cannot be compared with an exhibit set up in the hurly-burly and last minute problems of staging day.

BIBLE, PLANTS OF

Arrangers of church flowers, especially for flower festivals or saints' days, often need to know something of the plant material mentioned in Bible stories and texts. A Bible concordance is a great help in seeking texts which mention plant materials, perhaps for interpretation by arrangers. Concordances are available in most libraries and can be purchased in religious and other bookshops at various prices, depending on size.

Here are some of the better known Bible plants and plant products:

Bay tree	*Laurus nobilis*
Cedar of Lebanon	*Cedrus libani*, a giant spreading tree with fragrant red wood
Christ's thorns	*Paliurus spina-christi* and *Ziziphus spina-christi*
Frankincense	a resin from *Boswellia carteri*, *B. sacra* or *B. papyfera*
Gethsemane, Garden of	the name means 'the place of the oil press', and olives grew there
Lilies of the field	they are thought to have been *Anemone coronaria*, but the term may have referred to flowers generally and if so would have included the narcissus, iris, gladiolus, poppy, jasmine and red tulip
Manna	possibly the tamarisk shrub (*Tamarix gallica*) because aphids feeding on it exude a sweet resin. The other possibility is a lichen (*Lecanora*)
Myrrh	a yellow gum obtained from *Commiphora molmol* or *C. myrrha*, a spiky shrub grown in Arabia
Papyrus	a tall water reed (*Cyperus papyrus*). The pith was used in strips to make paper
Rose	it is generally agreed that this is not the rose we know, but probably the narcissus or the red tulip
Rose of Jerico	*Nerium oleander*, the oleander shrub
Spikenard	a sweet-smelling ointment made from the Himalayan valerian (*Nardostachys jatamansi*)
Tares	*Lolium temulentum*, darnel, a weed which looks like wheat when young

Plants of the Virgin Mary

Linked with Bible plants, and also useful for interpretative arrangements in church are the many plants associated with the Virgin Mary. The list is extensive, the popular names usually beginning 'Our Lady's or 'Lady's' . . . smock, keys, gloves, hair, mantle, bower, thimble, ribbons, bells, etc.

Perhaps the earliest and best known is the Madonna Lily (*Lilium candidum*) seen in countless Renaissance paintings of the Annunciation and symbolizing the purity of the Virgin. The rose has also been her flower for centuries, and Mary is sometimes called the Mystic Rose. In Renaissance paintings the blue iris stood for Mary as the Queen of Heaven. Rosemary (*Rosmarinus officinalis*) is the Virgin's flower too, although the 'Mary' part of the name comes from the botanical name which means 'dew of the sea'. The marigold or common calendula was 'Mary's Gold', and the bright rayed petals represented her golden halo.

The Virgin's plants were often grown in monastery 'Mary gardens', providing both medicinal and culinary herbs and flowers for decoration on her festival days. One of the best known gardens in Britain today is the Cloister Garden at Lincoln Cathedral which grows some 40 of the Virgin's flowers.

BIENNIALS

Plants which grow during the first year, then flower, fruit and die during the second year, e.g. honesty (*Lunaria annua*), Scotch thistle (*Onopordum*), many foxgloves (*Digitalis*) and wallflowers (*Cheiranthus*). For a succession of plants seeds must be sown each year.

BOILING STEM ENDS, *see* CONDITIONING

BOTANICAL NAMES

So many flower arrangers are scared of botanical names, shying away from them and relying on local or common names for plants. These common names, often centuries old, like lady's mantle, liverwort, foxglove and love-in-a-mist are evocative and attractive and will surely not die out. But they are not precise and what one part of the country calls 'cowslips' may be 'paigles' in another. What many people call Queen Anne's lace (*Anthriscus sylvestris*) has more than 50 local names!

In the eighteenth century, Linnaeus, a Swedish scholar, evolved a means of classifying all known plants. It was – and is, for it is still the basis of today's taxonomy – in Latin (and some Greek) and is known and accepted all over the world. Linnaeus classified each plant by its family, genus and species, sometimes with a further name to identify the variety or the cultivar, e.g.,

Family	Genus	Species	Variety or cultivar
Caprifoliaceae	*Viburnum*	*tinus*	'Variegatum'
Berberidaceae	*Berberis*	*thunbergii*	*atropurpurea*
Araliaceae	*Hedera*	*colchica*	*dentata* 'Variegata'

It is common practice to use a capital letter for the genus, and a small letter for the species and variety, unless it is in inverted commas, when it takes a capital. The family name is useful, but it is the last three names that truly identify a plant, so that you know exactly which is which – as would a correspondent in China, France or Brazil. The Linnaeus system is a truly international language.

Don't be abashed that you have little Latin. It won't matter desperately if you get an ending wrong and use 'aurea' instead of 'aureum' or 'aureus'. What matters is that you recognize the first part of the word as meaning 'golden' or 'yellow'. Understanding why a plant has some particular part of its name (*chinensis* = from China; *forsythia* was named after William Forsyth, a royal gardener; *foetidissima* – stinking; *spinosa* – spiny) helps a great deal if you are trying to recall the name when seeing the plant, or the plant when confronted with the name. It really is worth the trouble of learning the botanical names, so that you will not make the mistake of buying an *Arum italicum* when you want the marbled leaves of an *Arum italicum pictum*.

BUCKETS

Ordinary plastic household buckets are quite satisfactory for conditioning flowers, but sometimes the swing handles trap and damage precious flower heads. Invest in tall, side-handled flower buckets if you can. (*See* TOOLS & EQUIPMENT)

A useful and inexpensive carrier to keep buckets steady and upright in a car can be made from an inverted flower box or lid. Mark two circles a little larger than the bucket base and cut a star-shape from the centre of each, leaving the triangular flaps to secure the bucket, as in the diagram. (*See* **PACKING**)

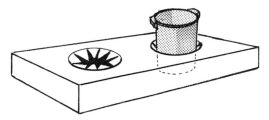

Buckets *An inexpensive bucket holder for the car made from a flower box.*

BULBS

Bulbs are complete underground food stores for a plant and strictly need nothing more than water, warmth and light to bring the plant to flowering. It is always sensible to grow the flowers and colours that one cannot easily buy, for example, the cottage, parrot and Rembrandt tulips; unusual double daffodils and tiny rockery ones; and the dainty Roman hyacinth (*Hyacinthus orientalis albulus*) or fritillarias.

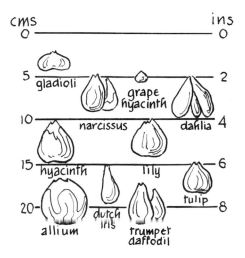

Bulbs *A planting diagram for garden bulbs.*

Prepared bulbs

For Christmas and the New Year bowls planted with prepared bulbs are as welcome as fresh indoor flowers. To bloom at Christmas they must be planted by mid-September. Choose a bowl without drainage holes and at least 10 cm (4 in.) deep (to allow the roots to develop) and fill with moist compost or bulb fibre. Plant the bulbs closely, nearly touching, with the noses just showing above the surface. Place the bowl in a cool, dark place for ten weeks. When the new leaves, pale cream at this stage, are about 3–5 cm (1–2 in.) high, bring the bowl gradually into more warmth and more light, and finally into the living-room. Water regularly and the bulbs will flower in four to five weeks. Covering the compost with moss or very fine chippings helps to keep it moist and look attractive.

BUYING FLOWERS

The best stage at which to buy flowers to ensure their longest possible life in an arrangement varies with different kinds.

Bulb flowers: buy when in bud, but with some petal colour already showing to be sure the flowers open. Buds that are too tight sometimes do not open at all.

Carnations: large single blooms should be almost fully open, but there should be no white 'threads' visible. If so, the flower is fully mature already. Spray carnations should have about one third to one half the flowers open or opening. The very tight green buds will usually come out, even several weeks later.

Daisy flowers: chrysanthemums, gerberas, etc.
  single types which have a definite centre should not have yellowish-orange pollen showing and the centres should be greenish and still tight.
  double types – avoid drooping or loose outer petals and look for a close centre.

Flower spikes: gladioli, delphiniums, freesias and shrub or tree blossoms should be bought when only one or two of the lower florets are open, so that there are plenty still to develop.

Roses: buy in bud, but not too tight; colour must be showing.

Tulips: if fresh the leaves 'squeak' when handled (see also **Bulb flowers** on previous page). As well as looking at the flower heads and buds, look at the stems and leaves. Both should be crisp and not discoloured, and should not have a slimy look nor smell stagnant.

General: wide open flowers can be a good buy if they are being sold off cheaply and are only wanted for a party, for instance. Any cut flower on sale at a florist's, market or stall should be standing in water, but if they are in full sunlight, near a radiator, on a draughty corner or where passers-by have brushed past them, their vase-life will already have been seriously shortened. While many retailers wrap the stems of cut flowers, it is really the heads that need protection. Get the flowers home as soon as possible, recut the stem ends and place in deep water in a cool place for an hour or two before arranging.

BYZANTINE (AD 395–1453)

This period is best known to arrangers for the **Byzantine cone** (q.v.). The Byzantine Empire was formed in AD 395 when the former Roman Empire divided in two and the eastern half was centred on the capital at Constantinople. Almost all Byzantine art – whether in the form of mosaics (one of the most important media), paintings or manuscripts – was religious in origin, so little that survives shows any detail of secular life at the time. Christianity was one of the chief influences, but art also reflected the luxury and the splendour of the Orient. Depicted figures are stylized and so are some of the plant forms and animals, but most are naturalistic enough to be recognizable.

Settings
Rounded arches and rounded vaulting in churches; pillars with infinitely varied capitals; mosaic decoration on floors, walls and ceilings; silken curtains; and ribbons wound round columns and garlands. The peacock is featured in various ways, and its tail feathers used decoratively.

Colours
White backgrounds in early mosaics, blue, aquamarine, scarlet red, viridian green, gold and peacock colours.

bowl of lotus (5th -Salonika

ceiling mosaic S.Giovanni 641AD

ewer circa 325 AD
mosaic at S.Vitale, Ravenna

stylised trees circa 1100 AD.

base of column of leaves & fruit in a basket (Ravenna)

Byzantine *Some features of Byzantine design (AD 395–1453).*

Flowers and plants
Mosaics and paintings portray the following identifiable trees and leaves – cypress, bay or laurel, ivy, myrtle, rosemary, pine, acanthus, vines, olive, palms and green swamp reed. Fruits include grapes, olives, citrus fruits, what appear to be apples or pears but may be peaches, and brilliant red fruit hanging in bunches. Flowers include white lilies, red roses and unidentified blue and purple flowers (anemones perhaps?). Vine tendrils and green and gold acanthus leaves curve and curl through many designs.

Containers
Low bowls, woven baskets, ewers or jugs appear in mosaics.

Arrangements and uses
Tall slender stylized columns of leaves with fruit, and sometimes flowers, coming from woven baskets, often end in a tapering point reflecting the curve of the arch. A mosaic at the Basilica Acheiropoietos in Salonika shows

a bowl of lotus in bud, leaf and flower and with its distinctive holed seed heads. Circular garlands of vines, wheatears, bay, lilies and fruits are shown in ceiling mosaics. (*See* **PERIOD ARRANGING**)

BYZANTINE CONE

To make a present-day cone-shaped decoration you will need:

container low dish, stemmed dish or tazza, urn.

mechanics a commercial cone-shape of floral foam either wet (green) or dry (brown), or one made from roughly-shaped blocks of foam, or a cone shape of 1–2 cm ($\frac{1}{2}$–$\frac{3}{4}$ in.) wire-netting filled with sphagnum moss. Mechanics must be securely wired or taped to the container. For fresh plant material the foam or moss should be well soaked.

plant materials short lengths only are needed (5–6 cm (2–$2\frac{1}{4}$ in.)) unless the cone is very big. Bushy foliage (box, holly, cupressus) or 'rosette'-shaped sprigs (skimmia, choisya) are useful for covering the mechanics. Flowers, fruits, cones, baubles, ribbon bows, etc. can then be added either at random or in spirals. Dried and preserved foliage will almost certainly need to be given a wire stem, and soft-stemmed fresh material may need a hole with a skewer or cocktail stick. Spear fruits with cocktail sticks.

Note: The top of the cone dries out quickly. Frequent mist-spraying helps to reduce this.

Byzantine Cone *A present day Byzantine cone of evergreens, fruit and flowers.*

CANDLE CUP

This is a metal or plastic cup or small bowl with a spigot to fit into a candlestick, bottle or very narrow-necked vase. Fix it in firmly with putty-type adhesive. The cup is best used with a round of floral foam which should protrude above the cup by about 2 cm ($\frac{3}{4}$ in.) to allow stems to be inserted at the sides as well as the top. Secure the foam with tape or a cap of 2 cm ($\frac{3}{4}$ in.) mesh wired round the cup and candlestick or vase. (*See* **MECHANICS** diagram on page 115)

Cups can be bought in black, white and metallic finishes and can be painted to match the container.

CANDLES

Candles are the arranger's most popular accessories, especially at Christmas and party time. They can be included in the actual arrangement or grouped with it in separate candlesticks or candelabra.

Buying and fixing

When buying candles check that they are straight and have no hair-cracks, which are impossible to mend. Fix the candles securely to ensure that they are absolutely vertical; tilted candles are distracting and burn unevenly. If the candles are to be in floral foam you can fix them in purchased holders (see diagrams) or, tape four cocktail sticks to the bottom of the candle and push these into the foam. If greater height or strength is needed use kebab sticks instead cut to the length needed. Candles in candlesticks or bottles can be secured with Plasticine or Oasis-fix or by winding several layers of clear adhesive tape loosely round the bottom of the candle to wedge it firmly into the socket.

fixing candles

taped cocktail sticks for use in foam

holders for use in pinholders or foam

spike holder for large candles

aerosol spray tops can be used

If candles are not going to be lit (as for a show) lift the wicks upright and trim them neatly with sharp scissors. The wicks can also be glittered at Christmas or given a false ribbon or paper 'flame'.

Candles *Inexpensive cherub candle-holders used at different heights for extra interest. The lower one is fitted with a candle-cup and floral foam to hold the flowers.*

General tips

Choose the colour carefully to link with the linen or tableware, or the occasion, e.g., ruby wedding or Easter.

Tall candles provide contrasting verticals on a laid table, so be generous with their length.

If using two or three candles within an arrangement, have the heights slightly unequal. Slice a little off one with a hot knife or raise one on 'legs'.

Remember, candles give a dim yellowish light. Dark colours will look black and appear to be 'holes' in the arrangement, so concentrate on paler tints, lime-green, white and yellow for the best effects.

Generally, plain candles look best with flower arrangements which are fussy in themselves. The clean, smooth lines provide an excellent contrast.

WARNING: *Risk of fire*. Candles which are to be lit must be kept well away from plant material, especially dried and artificial. Never leave candles alight in an arrangement after a meal is over and everyone is leaving the room.

CARPETS, FLORAL

Floral carpets are guaranteed show-stoppers at festivals in churches or stately homes. They have the advantage of involving a good number of people, and, once the design and mechanics have been worked out, do not demand a high degree of skill from the arrangers. The designing, planning and organization, however, are crucial. The design must be created first to fit the size desired or laid down. The mechanics are usually plastic seed, or foil cooking, trays filled with blocks of floral foam, so the pattern is divided and graphed into X number of units. Each unit and each tray must be numbered, and a tissue pattern drawn for each tray showing the shapes and colours to be used.

The grid pattern and numbers can be marked out in chalk on the floor if this is possible. If not, and the floor must be protected, then mark the grid on polythene sheets. When the completed trays start coming in be careful to lay them *in situ*, starting at one end or in the middle, working towards the outside.

Finish off with ribbon and fringes to hide the sides of the trays. Spray thoroughly.

A carpet about 6×3 m ($6\frac{1}{2} \times 3\frac{1}{4}$ yd) will take a great deal of foliage of different shades and some 5,000 or more flower heads.

CHINESE (AD 960–1912)

Although China had traded with Mediterranean countries and the west since Roman times and had produced works of the highest artistic quality,

Chinese features and arrangements (960–1912).

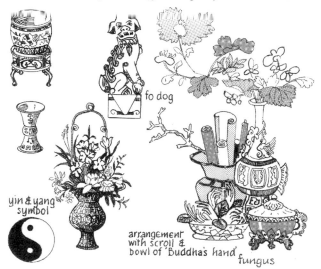

fo dog

yin & yang symbol

arrangement with scroll & bowl of 'Buddha's hand' fungus

'the flowery kingdom' remained unknown and untouched by western ideas until after 1912. An agricultural country of huge size and therefore with many different climates and landscapes, it had a rigid social structure and three major religious and philosophical influences, Confucianism, Buddhism and Taoism. Each stressed the one-ness of man with nature and, variously, the value of contemplation, simplicity and the preservation of life in all its forms, including plants. Gardens were small-scale replicas of the natural landscape. The flower and garden arts ranked with painting and music as a cultural expression.

Settings
Houses and pagodas with characteristic upturned eaves; columns of vermilion red; tiled floors with bamboo mats; lacquered furniture in red, black and gold; dark woods inlaid with mother-of-pearl; screens; and hanging wall scrolls.

Colours
Yellow was the imperial colour worn by the Emperor; red, the mandarin's colour, was the colour of happiness and used for weddings and festivals; white was the colour of mourning.

Plant materials
The peony was the king of flowers; pine, bamboo and plum blossom were the 'three friends of the cold season'; other important flowers were peach, apricot, cherry, quince and magnolia blossom; chrysanthemum, iris, lotus (Buddha's flower), orchid, narcissus, azalea, rose, wisteria, lilac and grasses. Peaches, pomegranates, gourds and citron (the Buddha's hand fungus) were also featured.

Containers and bases
All Chinese vases had their own carved wood base or stand. Early containers were bronze ritual vessels, later copied in porcelain, enamel and cloissoné. Generally, metal was used for winter and spring, and porcelain for summer and autumn. Shapes were immensely varied, and most vases were decorated with patterns. Baskets were widely used in many shapes.

Arrangements and uses
Like **ikebana**, (q.v.) arrangements are asymmetrical, but there are no rules about stem lengths and angles. Flowers and branches are arranged as naturalistically as possible and from the same season and environment; no more than three different kinds or colours are used in one vase, and odd numbers are preferred. The vase is always important and the colour should be in *contrast* to the flowers.

   To the Chinese the time, situation and setting was important for the full enjoyment of flowers. Arrangements stood on low tables, chests or on the floor. They are often shown grouped together at different heights, or with a group of accessories, linked, as in a western still life, by an association of ideas.

Symbolism
Taoist folklore has given symbolism and meanings to most plants in common use; they are often linked with the seasons and also with birds. The lotus, for example, signifies summer, as well as nobility and purity, and is

linked with mandarin ducks for marital bliss and the egret for purity.

The *yang* (white) and *yin* (black) Taoist concept of the positive and negative forces of the cosmos is also related to flowers and leaves. (*See* **PERIOD ARRANGING**)

CHRISTMAS DECORATIONS

Everyone loves decorations at Christmas time and today we are spoiled for choice of materials with the range of long-lasting gold, silver, copper and pearly finishes to plastic flowers and leaves. Metallic paint-sprays are such an improvement on the old paint that used to tarnish before Christmas was over; brilliant lacquered fruits and berries can be stored for use year after year; baubles are now unbreakable; tree lights sparkle in all shapes and sizes; glitter and snow can now be sprayed on evergreens; ribbons come in all colours and widths and are waterproof; and polyester flowers are almost as good as the real thing. The problem is in selection. Decide, in good time, what your scheme for next Christmas is going to be and work towards that end.

Where to decorate

Don't spread your decorations too much but concentrate them. Will it be at the entrance, in the hall, stairway, dining-room, sitting-room or lounge, den/study, kitchen or upstair landing? Choose to decorate what suits you, your home, your family and your purse.

Plant materials

If you are a purist you will want all fresh plant material: the traditional evergreens of holly, ivy, fir, pine, yew, bay and rosemary, with cones and fruit and poinsettias, chrysanthemums, carnations, etc. from the florist.

Alternatively, you may go for the less time-consuming artificial 'greens' and flowers, perhaps in traditional colours or the more unusual pink, turquoise, apricot or pearly look.

Most arrangers will want to use both natural and artificial, for Christmas is a time when it all goes together – fresh, dried, painted, plastic, glittered, polyester, paper, ribbon, tinsel and lacquer.

Choosing a style

It is temptingly easy, but very dull, to do the same thing each Christmas, even if the family expects some traditional things. Try at least one new idea and re-vamp some of the old ones each year. Recently the one-colour theme has become popular, especially for the decoration of the tree, with lights, baubles, bows, parcels and other hangings all in gold, or white and silver, red or whatever colour you choose. This can be carried through to other decorations too, but the result is somewhat sophisticated and perhaps not for a home where there are lots of children who like bright, mixed colours.

The Victorian revival extends to more than just Christmas cards and wrapping paper. In Dickensian spirit, the Christmas dinner-table decked out with epergne and garlands looks very splendid, though not everyone will want to return to paper chains and real candles clipped onto the tree branches!

For the very modern home driftwood, bold seedheads and dried leaves can be given a touch of gold spray and glitter and arranged with poinsettias and baubles in more sparse modern styles. A pot-et-fleur in a large planter needs only a few red flowers added to look Christmassy. Staircases, being the

Christmas *Ideas for Christmas: (top, left to right) kissing bough, swag of floral woven mats on wide ribbon, snowy log with robin and candles; (centre) winter landscape, door wreath of evergreens with apples and cones, 3-D Christmas card; (bottom) choir boys with lantern, wine bottle candleholder with collar of flowers and foliage, a stylized garland tree with ribbons.*

Christmas *The magic of candle-light at Christmas time. The artificial plant materials and candles are in a block of dry foam taped securely to the head.*

central point of most homes, look very effective decorated with garlanding and bows.

For those arrangers who are nimble-fingered there are many craft items to attempt: cards, calendars and gift-tags with pressed or artificial flowers and leaves; decorated parcels; crackers, place mats, napkin rings, menu or place name holders for the table; angels, Father Christmases, snowmen, robins and so on. (*See* ***colour section***)

Pointers for success
1 Several large arrangements or features are worth a dozen fiddly ones dotted about. If interest is focussed, the impact is greater.
2 Be as lavish as your pocket will allow. One candle looks lonely and weak; three are better; a dozen begins to look sumptuous. The same applies to baubles and tree lights. If it can't all be afforded in one year, plan to build up items next year.
3 Make sure, in good time, that you have to hand what you may need. It is a good idea to load a tray (or trolley if you can spare it) with all the Christmas things when you are ready to start work on the decorations.
   You're likely to need:

flower cutters	nylon fishing line (for invisible
household scissors	hanging)
craft knife	white liquid shoe cleaner (substitute
adhesives	snow)
paint sprays: metallic, snow,	candles
glitter	paper napkins
cleaning solvent	crêpe paper (foil and other)
stem-binding tape	wrapping papers
clear adhesive tape	beads
ribbons (chosen colours)	sequins
baubles	stamens
cones, assorted sizes	drawing pins
plastic leaf sprays (for making	
into smaller units)	

4 Do detailed work well in advance. Make paper/ribbon flowers, wire cones and baubles, wire up small sprays from larger plastic ones, make and wire ribbon loops and curls. If you make up a whole artificial decoration well before Christmas, put it right away in a box or plastic bag or you will be sick of the sight of it by Christmas time.
5 Although it is tempting in the New Year to put away arrangements as they are, do take them apart and store the components separately, ready for next year's look and new inspiration.

CHURCH FLOWERS

Arranging flowers for church should be an enjoyable occupation, but one approached with reverence. Arrangers should use their skills and plant materials to best effect, but not to gain personal acclaim. This is true of routine arranging as part of the weekly flower rota and for special occasions and festivals.

Flower arrangements in church must never be in the way of the clergy, choir, organist or bell-ringers or impede the conduct of services; the clergy's wishes or rules about flowers must always be respected; monuments, tablets, brasses, etc. should never be obscured and nails or other fixings must never be driven in without permission.

The principal difference between flowers in church and in the home is one of scale. In church the distances are greater, the furnishings larger and the light often dimmer than at home. Arrangements need to be bolder, fairly light in colour and clear in outline as they are seen most often from a distance. Fussy, fiddly arrangements are out of place except where they may be seen close to, as at the font or in a side chapel for private prayer.

Choice of plant material

Choose flowers that are simple and bold in outline and luminous in colouring: yellow, orange, clear red and all the paler tints such as cream, pink, mauve, apricot, pale blue and lime green. These will show up in poor light. Daisy shapes (chrysanthemums, gerberas), strong spikes (delphiniums, eremurus, gladioli, foxgloves and branches of blossom), bell shapes (lilies, daffodils, tulips), and round flowers (roses, hydrangeas, dahlias, peonies) are good choices.

Foliage may be varied and mixed, but it is usually better to keep to, say, three different types in one arrangement, chosen for contrast of form and texture and some variation in colour. Leaves with white, yellow or lime-green variegation are useful to help lighten arrangements, and grey foliage is effective with some colour schemes. Choose flowers and leaves that will last at least a week because withered arrangements in church (or anywhere else) look sad, uncared for and much worse than no arrangement at all.

The flower rota

The newcomer asked to join the church flower rota and do the flowers for the first time is often daunted by not knowing the ropes. Churches or flower rota organizers should provide arrangers with a sheet giving the following necessary information:

1 The days/times when the flowers can be done.
2 When the church will be locked and where the key is.
3 Whether the arranger supplies (a) foliage and (b) flowers. Whether she is expected to pay for and donate the flowers (usual in most small churches) or to claim an allowance from a flower fund.
4 What positions the flowers needed are in.
5 Whether containers and mechanics are provided, and if so where they are stored.
6 Where the water supply is and where to put rubbish.
7 What to do with the previous week's flowers.
8 Whether the arranger is expected to look after the arrangements throughout the week or whether that is the task of another volunteer.

Since nothing is more frustrating than arriving to do the flowers and finding you lack some essential item, aim to be prepared and take with you.

Tools flower cutters, scissors or secateurs; newspapers or a drop sheet to work on and collect rubbish; misting spray; long-spouted water can; cloths for mopping up; brush and dust pan; and a large plastic rubbish bag.

Mechanics flower foam or wire mesh, reel wire, string or tape to secure the mechanics; plastic cones and sticks for a tall arrangement.

Plant materials well-conditioned, long lasting flowers and foliage. Take them in buckets if there are many arrangements to do and they have to be out of water for any length of time.

Remember that cleaning up from the previous week's arrangements, and setting up new mechanics often takes far longer than one expects. Tidy up and leave everything spick and span and check that containers are topped up (but not over-flowing). If you give arrangements a final mist spray, be careful not to mark polished wood or altar cloths.

Pot-et-fleur
In most churches fresh flower and foliage arrangements are preferred throughout the year, so it is surprising that more use is not made of **pot-et-fleur** (q.v.), which are houseplants grouped or planted in large containers and highlighted with a few colourful cut flowers. These long lasting display features need good maintenance, of course, but are less work and far better value for money in the winter months.

Dried and preserved materials
Foliage preserved with glycerine makes an excellent standby for church arranging as do many of the larger dried flowers and seedheads, especially hydrangeas, Chinese lanterns (*Physalis alkekengie* or *P. franchettii*), pampas grass, teasels, bulrushes, honesty (*Lunaria annua*), allium, cardoon or artichoke and achillea. It is important that they are not left to get dusty, battered and neglected-looking; re-arrange and refurbish frequently.

Altar
Not all churches have flowers *on* the altar, but when they are permitted, arrangements should never dominate the cross, but lead the eye towards it. Because of the customary symmetrical arrangement of a central cross and flanking candlesticks, a pair of altar vases is usual. In Anglican and non-conformist churches, however, the altar is often a table, which the clergy officiate behind; flowers are then not always very suitable and need to be kept low.

Many altar vases are notoriously difficult to arrange in because of their narrow necks, but floral foams help. For a pair of vases, divide the flowers and foliage into two, allocating to the right or the left stems and branches which have a natural bend in that direction. Remember that each vase is not exactly like the other but a 'mirror image' with features on the right of one, placed left in the other.

If there is a reredos immediately behind the altar and it is ornately carved, a mosaic, a painting or an elaborate tapestry or embroidery, it may be useful to use some 'solid' foliage such as laurel, magnolia or beech to make a plainer background against which the flowers can be better seen.

If in any doubt, check what the colour of the altar frontal will be before ordering/picking flowers. The liturgical colours in Christian churches are:

Celebration	Liturgical colours
Advent	purple or dark blue (flowers are not always allowed)
Christmas and Festival of Epiphany	white and gold
Epiphany (5 Sundays)	green
Lent and 3 Sundays before Easter	purple or dark blue (often no flowers are allowed except, perhaps, for weddings)
Holy Week (except Good Friday)	gold
Good Friday	black
Easter until Whitsun	white and gold
Whitsunday	red
Trinity Sunday	gold
Next 22 Sundays in Trinity	green
Martyrs' days	red
All festivals, weddings, Saints' days	white and gold

The altar flowers are the most important of all and the best blooms should be chosen for them. If flowers are not to be actually *on* the altar, it is usual to have one pedestal, or a pair, standing nearby. Although they will be seen only from a distance by most of the congregation, raised as high as possible, their colour and beauty will add much to the enjoyment of the service.

Altar flowers, especially a pair of vases, are best arranged *in situ*, but meticulous care must be taken to protect the altar cloths and the carpet with plastic sheeting. When arranging, walk once or twice to the back of the church, checking how the vases look at various distances. When the arrangements are finished, top up the water and mist spray if you are able to without damaging anything nearby. Leave the surroundings immaculate.

Font

Decorating the font for christenings must be done with care so that the ceremony is in no way hampered. The incumbent must be consulted.

It is pretty to garland or decorate the top with posies as long as the flowers are kept low and a wide space is left at the 'back' for the vicar/priest and the baby! Small arrangements can usually go round the base provided they do not protrude as people usually gather closely round the font for a christening.

Choose fairly small unsophisticated flowers and arrange them as a continuing circlet in damp moss, or small sausages of floral foam laid on a strip of plastic. Alternatively, use small, shallow dishes for little posy arrangements linked with trails of ivy or fern. The essentials are simplicity, neatness and attention to detail, as the flowers will be seen very close to. Spring flowers are especially pretty for this kind of decoration, but small roses, sprigs of delphinium, spray carnations and gypsophila are attractive in summer, and in autumn berries, pom-pom dahlias and Michaelmas daisies can be used. The traditional 'blue for a boy, pink for a girl' can be followed, but any pastel colour or all-white is pretty.

Pedestals

Pedestal arrangements are especially useful and effective in church for two reasons. First, they can stand wherever needed in a convenient space and be moved from place to place – with care and a stalwart helper – even after the arrangement is done! Secondly, they raise the flowers above the heads of the seated congregation and can be seen from a distance. (*See also* PEDESTALS)

Pew ends

For festivals, weddings and special occasions no other decoration gives the effect of a church filled with flowers for so little outlay.

mechanics for pew ends

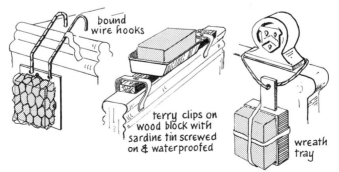

bound wire hooks

terry clips on wood block with sardine tin screwed on & waterproofed

wreath tray

The mechanics will vary according to the shape of the pew end (see diagrams) and in a church where the central aisle is narrow it is essential to keep the decorations small and neat. Trails of ivy or fern, or coloured and curled ribbon streamers will give them more importance. For convenience, decorations that hang from the pew can be arranged on a work-table but when they are put in place be prepared for them to drip for a time and expect to have to make one or two final adjustments owing to the angle of viewing. It is not usually necessary to decorate every pew end but every alternate, or every third row, staggering them on either side of the aisle.

Pillars
Pillars are usually decorated only for special festivals and then they are often garlanded spirally or hung with swags or plaques. These can usually be from wire or nylon fishing line, secured out of sight round the capital. Sometimes there is a convenient high ledge to hold containers for trailing, waterfall arrangements. Pedestals can often be placed backing onto pillars which provide a neutral colour setting for the flowers. It is economical, too, because there is no need for plant material at the back. A column of flowers against a pillar can be constructed with the mechanics shown on page 117.

Porches
Welcoming flowers in the porch are always appreciated and there is usually room somewhere on a window ledge, stone seat or in a corner for a bright, cheerful arrangement. Baskets are pretty and informal here if there is room.

Decorative topiary trees or tall cones of foliage are attractive outside the church entrance, at the gate or flanking the path for weddings and festivals.

Pulpit
Because the pulpit is in a prominent position it seems to be felt that flowers are needed somewhere here. If there is a ledge or niche to take container(s) then some decoration is possible, but the top is seldom a suitable place for flowers and they are likely to be a nuisance there. Many pulpits are carved and decorative in themselves and need little extra. It is sad to see wooden

Church Flowers *Various features for church windows: (1) with strong light from behind, make a fairly dense backing of leaves (2) a tracery of branches or flowers will be attractive in silhouette; (3) a wedge to take a container on a sloping sill; (4) a central arrangement; (5) asymmetric arrangements against the embrasure at either side of the window.*

panelling or carving marked with water stains from attempts to hang fresh swags or garlands, and they should only be made if staining can be avoided.

Windows

Window decorations have much to commend them for the flowers are usually high enough to be seen and they are out of the way of the congregation. Against this they can pose several problems:

- the light comes from behind the flowers
- the sill slopes
- they are high up and difficult to get at

The first can be dealt with in two ways. One can make a fairly solid backing of leaves such as laurel, rhododendron or aucuba and arrange the flowers in front of them, or use branches or lacy flowers to make a tracery so that the outline provides interest when seen in silhouette. Pussy willow (*Salix caprea*), budding horse chestnut branches (*Aesculus hippocastanum*) and Queen Anne's lace (*Anthriscus sylvestris*) are useful for this. When the glass is stained, far less light comes through, and it is usually possible to keep the flowers below any important part of the picture or text.

If the window sill slopes the most satisfactory answer is to have a wedge-shaped platform made on which a container can stand. The wedge can often be fitted to stand firmly on a narrow ledge; if not, the platform, or a tin container with holes drilled under the back rim to take wire or string, can be tied to a bar or catch of the window. String and tin will both be hidden by the arrangement.

High window arrangements can be tiring to do *in situ*. It is sensible to do most of the arrangement on a table nearby, perhaps trying it on the sill (with a proper step-ladder, instead of wobbling on a chair) just once to gauge the height and angle from which it will be seen. When almost complete the arrangement can be put in place, the finishing touches made and the water topped up.

For a window at any height, few containers are more satisfactory than a low trough – a bread, baking or chicken-feed tin – or a casserole dish. The tin can be painted matt black, grey or darkish green so that it will not be seen. Use crumpled 5 cm (2 in.) mesh wire netting or water-retaining foam as mechanics. About half a standard block of foam would be enough, but it *must* protrude above the container by at least a cm (½ in.) so that stems can be angled down over the sill and sideways. A cap of 2 cm (¾ in.) mesh tied over the foam gives extra support, and if the tin tends to tip forward, weight it with lead strips bent over the back rim or partly fill it with stones or pebbles.

Depending on the situation of the window and the angle from which it will be seen by the congregation, arrangements can be central, on one side or on both sides, when it is better to have them asymmetrical with one side taller and larger and the other lower and smaller. High windows look better with some of the arrangement flowing over the sill. At harvest time windows are often decorated across the full width with fruits and vegetables, but there should be some higher feature to the arrangement to give a focus of interest.

A window arrangement can look very different in the morning with the sun behind it and in the evening when it is dark outside and the church lights are on. If it is possible check your handiwork under both conditions.

(*See* **FLORAL CARPETS, FLOWER FESTIVALS, PEDESTALS, POT-ET-FLEUR, WEDDING FLOWERS**)

CITY AND GUILDS

The City and Guilds of London Institute, founded in 1878, is an independent examining body working closely with industry and the education service. It sets syllabuses, examines and issues certificates which establish a nationally recognized standard for a vast range of subjects, including many practical and vocational ones. The courses for these examinations are mostly run by colleges of technology and adult education.

There are certificates available at two levels in flower arrangement (No. 7900) and in floristry (No. 019) which normally cover three years of study for approximately one day a week. Acceptance for the third year is usually dependent on the satisfactory completion of Part I of the course. No qualification is necessary for embarking on a flower arrangement course – indeed it is planned for beginners – but the floristry course is intended for those already employed in the trade.

Flower arrangement includes a comprehensive study of all aspects of flower arrangement, including design, show work, festival organization, period and modern styles as well as botany and horticulture. It covers theory and practical work.

Also of interest to arrangers who wish to teach is the City and Guilds Further Education Teachers' Certificate (No. 730). (*See* **APPENDIX: ADDRESSES**)

CLASSES

In most areas it is not difficult to find a local class in flower arrangement, and it is worth enquiring about any being run by the local education authority at adult education centres. Local flower clubs also organize short courses for their beginners and new members or day schools/workshops for more experienced members. Both the W.I. (Woman's Institute) and T.W.G. (Townswomen's Guild) also run courses from time to time. Sometimes a local flower arrangement teacher gives lessons in her own home, and the flower club should have information about that.

If you need a more 'in depth' or floristry course, there are the City and Guilds' certificate courses at some colleges of technology or adult education. (*See* **DAY SCHOOLS** or **WORKSHOPS**)

COCKTAIL STICKS

Known as toothpicks in America, these are useful for taping to the base of candles to be fixed in **floral foams** (q.v.) and for anchoring fruits, either to foam or to each other. Sometimes they are useful inserted into the bottom of hollow or soft stems to help bore a hole into foam. A pack of sticks should be in every arranger's work/tool box.

COLLAGE

The name comes from the French *coller*, which means 'to stick'. A collage is a picture or a decorative feature made by sticking all kinds of things to a background. It may be two- or three-dimensional.

Pressed flower pictures, scrapbooks, photomontage and Victorian scrap screens are all types of collage. In the British Museum are the exquisite 'paper mosaics' of flowers and plants made by Mrs Delany in the eighteenth

Collage Top: *seed collage of a section through a teasel seedhead.* Bottom: *a Victorian-style text in seeds of giant hogweed, decorated with pressed flowers and leaves.*

century. Early in the twentieth century, artists began to include collage in their pictures, and a large colourful one by Henri Matisse, known as *The Snail*, can be seen in the Tate Gallery, London.

The word 'collage' was not generally used until this century, and so has sometimes been associated more with abstract and free-style designs than with traditional pretty pictures, but today the term is all-embracing. In flower arrangement it may include pressed flower pictures, plaques and seed collages. These may actually represent flowers and plants or be made *of* plant materials to represent birds, animals, landscapes or purely abstract patterns.

This decorative technique has been used effectively by flower arrangers to create backgrounds for competitive work, heraldic shields and coats-of-arms, altar frontals, samplers, bell-pulls and large wall panels, usually in a combination of pressed and dried plant materials, with seeds and perhaps other non-plant forms, making them what is known as 'mixed media' collages. Greetings cards, gift tags and calendars are usually made from just pressed plant materials so that they can be sealed with a transparent self-adhesive plastic.

COLOUR

Colour is such a vital, and emotive, factor in flower arrangement that it is essential to have a working knowledge of colour and its vocabulary. It is not enough to be able to recite the rainbow colours – red, orange, yellow, green, blue, indigo and violet – or to remember the mnemonic 'Richard of York gained battles in vain' to help get them in the right order. We live in a colour-conscious world and should be able to use colours deliberately in arrangements to create the best effect for their setting or purpose.

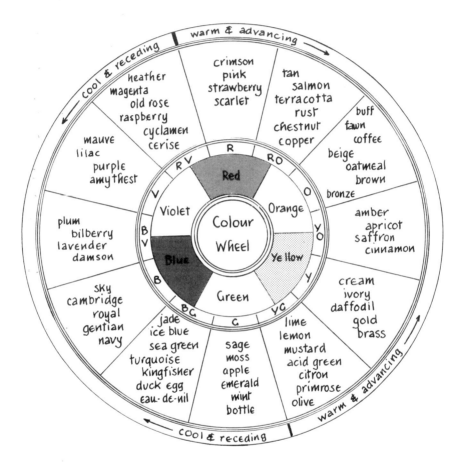

Colour *The colour wheel shows, at the centre, the primary and secondary hues, then the tertiary colours with segments giving the popular colour names which fall roughly within each. Perhaps the hardest to understand is that brown, from palest beige to darkest coffee, derives from the secondary colour, orange.*

The colour wheel

For convenience, artists devised the colour wheel (leaving out indigo) to show the natural sequence of hues and how colours can be combined and modified to make other colours, tints and shades.

Red, Yellow and Blue	the three primary colours from which all others can be made
Orange, Green and Violet	the three secondaries made from mixing red with yellow, yellow with blue and blue with red
Red-Orange, Yellow-Orange, Yellow-Green, Blue-Green, etc.	the tertiary colors – the in-betweens – slotting between the primaries and secondaries and made from both

ADD BLACK to any colour to give a *SHADE*
ADD WHITE to any colour to give a *TINT* (the so-called pastels)
ADD GREY to make a *TONE*

Black, white and grey are the neutral or achromatic colours, darkening or lightening the rainbow hues. Because we tend to speak of colours by more familiar names and say 'olive' rather than 'yellow-green' or 'pink' rather than a 'tint of red', the colour wheel on page 42 shows colours by their more colloquial names, but in the sector in which they belong.

The grouping of colours is easily understood by looking at a colour wheel. These are the categories:

Analogous (or adjacent) colours lie next to each other in the wheel and will have a 'parent' primary or secondary colour present in them. This makes it easy on the eye to group flowers of these colours and all their various tints, tones and shades together.

Complementary colours, on the contrary, lie opposite each other on the wheel and contain no common 'parent' colour. In full value, they are brightly contrasting, harsh even, and difficult to manage in an arrangement. But the interest lies in combining tints and shades of complementary colours for example dark blue with pale apricot, bottle green with pink, tan with eau-de-nil or deep crimson with pale sage-green. (See *colour section*.)

Monochromatic means all the tints, tones and shades of one colour, not necessarily just of grey or brown.

Polychromatic is multicoloured.

Light and colour

If the foregoing terms are understood, little other colour phraseology is really needed, but it is important to understand also what is meant by warm and cool, or advancing and receding colours. There is really no need to do more than look at them. Do the blues and purples make you feel chilly? Do the yellows, oranges and reds make you think of the sun and fire and warm you up again? Half close your eyes and look around the room. White paper will show up clearly, yellows will glow and pastel colours of any hue will show up, but black, purple, blue and green, especially the darker shades, will scarcely be visible as separate colours. This is what happens when the light begins to fail in the evening or in the dark corners of a room or church. The quality of showing up well in poor light is 'luminosity' and one needs to choose the more luminous colours and tints when selecting flowers for decorations late in the day or where light is poor. By contrast, very bright sunlight can 'bleach out' colour, rather like an over-exposed photograph, and then stronger hues are needed.

Artificial lighting affects colour in various ways:

Electric-tungsten (the usual household lighting)	red, orange, yellow are enhanced but blues and purples are deadened
Electric-fluorescent strip	blue and purple become vibrant, reds muddied to brown, yellows are neutralized
Candlelight	much the same effect as tungsten but candle-light is much dimmer. Blues, purples and dark greens – even dark reds – look black

Red	Orange	Yellow	Green	Blue	Violet

Sunlight spreads its energy fairly evenly

Tungsten light favours the red end of the spectrum

Fluorescent light enhances blue, violet & some greens

Colour associations

For interpretative arranging, colour makes considerable impact. It is the first thing most people notice and recall: the woman in the red coat, the house with the yellow front door, the pretty pink arrangement in the corner, the green car, and so on. Colours also have associations commonly understood within our own society or culture but they may differ in others: weddings may mean white to twentieth-century Britons, but to first-century Romans the wedding colour was saffron yellow. For us black is the colour of mourning, but in India it is white. National flag colours have come to represent many countries in sport and athletics; purple has been a royal colour for centuries because in early days the dye was so rare and expensive only the king could afford it.

Some of the better known colour associations, at least in the western hemisphere, are:

Red danger, fire, heat, passion, courage, war, violence, anger, guilt, communism, ruby wedding anniversary (40th), St Valentine, love, martyrdom, Christmas (with green).

phrases: red for danger, red-letter day, in the red (debt), red tape, caught red-handed, red rag to a bull.

Orange warmth, setting sun, autumn, vigour, Holland (House of Orange), Hallowe'en, 1930s.

phrases: curiously, there are no common phrases based on orange.

Yellow sun, springtime, happiness, Easter, wealth (as gold), golden wedding anniversary (50th), caution, cowardice, sickness, avarice.

phrases: gold-digger, Golden Age, gild the lily, heart of gold, brassy blonde, yellow-bellied.

Green youth and immaturity, nature, freshness, Ireland (Emerald Isle), jealousy, envy, restfulness, Christmas (with red).

phrases: green with envy, green fingers/thumbs.

Blue sea, cold, space (sky), calm, truth, serenity, the Virgin Mary, Oxford and Cambridge Universities, quality, intensity, conservatism, restraint.

phrases: blue with cold, blue for a boy, out of the blue, the blues (depression), deep blue sea, blue ribbon, 'something blue' (for brides).

Violet/purple royalty, richness, splendour, mourning.

phrases: purple prose, born to the purple, purple with rage.

Black death, mourning, night, evil, disaster, bad luck, witchcraft, piracy.

phrases: black as night/coal, in the black (solvent), black-hearted, black sheep, black mark, black look.

Brown autumn, sun tan, age.

phrases: in a brown study, browned off, brown as a berry, browned with age.

Grey/silver age, experience, penitence, half-mourning, fear, silver anniversary (25th), distance.

phrases: grey matter, silver lining, silver-tongued.

White purity, cleanliness, chastity, innocence, snow, luminosity, chalky, winter.

phrases: white as snow/as a sheet, white heat, white line, white elephant, white flag.

(*See also* liturgical colours under CHURCH FLOWERS, and ZODIAC)

COMMENT CARDS

Cards left by exhibits after **judging** (q.v.) to help competitors realize their mistakes and to encourage them for future shows. Known to judges by the three 'C's, they should provide comment and constructive criticism. Card writing is an important facet of the judge's work, both to help exhibitors and to indicate to the viewing public why decisions have been made.

CONDITIONING

Conditioning is the term used by flower arrangers for the preparation of cut flowers and leaves, *before* arranging them, to prolong their vase-life.

Essentially, conditioning means getting water up into the stems, leaves and flowers as soon as possible after the natural supply from the plant roots has been cut off. Deprived of water, flowers and leaves wilt, but they do not die immediately and can be revived before they start to shrivel.

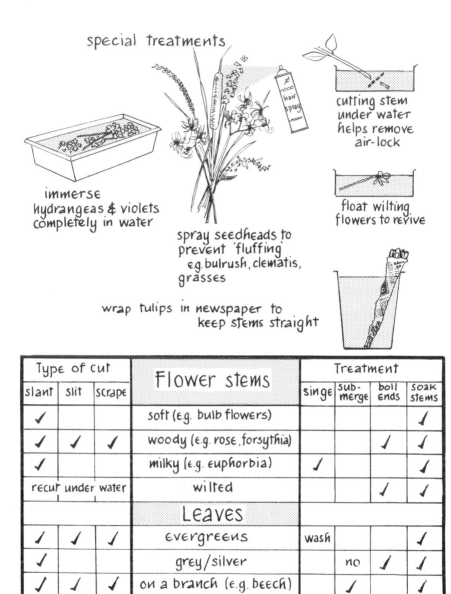

special treatments

immerse hydrangeas & violets completely in water

spray seedheads to prevent 'fluffing' e.g. bulrush, clematis, grasses

wrap tulips in newspaper to keep stems straight

cutting stem under water helps remove air-lock

float wilting flowers to revive

Type of cut			Flower stems	Treatment			
slant	slit	scrape		singe	sub-merge	boil ends	soak stems
✓			soft (e.g. bulb flowers)				✓
✓	✓	✓	woody (e.g. rose, forsythia)			✓	✓
✓			milky (e.g. euphorbia)	✓			✓
recut under water			wilted			✓	✓
			Leaves				
✓	✓	✓	evergreens	wash			✓
✓			grey/silver		no	✓	✓
✓	✓	✓	on a branch (e.g. beech)		✓		✓
✓	✓	✓	tender & new		no	✓	✓
✓			single (ivy, fatsia)		✓		

Cutting and trimming

1 When cutting from the garden choose the cool of the day and take a bucket of water, rather than a basket, and put the stems into water at once.

2 Cut all stems on a slant to give a greater area for water up-take.

3 Slit thick woody stems and scrape away the outer bark for 2–5 cm ($\frac{3}{4}$–2 in.), for the same reason.

4 If cut stems have dried out as you take them home from a country walk or from the florist, recut them (to remove any 'scab' tissue) before placing in water.

5 Trim away thorns, snags, and bitten, mis-shapen or crowded leaves and any that are likely to be underwater in the final arrangement.

The long drink/soaking

Allow cut flowers and leaves to stand at least two hours, and preferably overnight, in deep water in a cool place so that they are fully turgid before you arrange them. At this stage add any substance to prolong cut-flower life if you want to. (*See* ADDITIVES)

Submerge leaves, except grey ones, for the same period, but for very young immature leaves half an hour is enough or they become saturated and brown.

Shock treatments

Boiling: foliage sprays, flowers with woody stems (roses, blossom, hydrangeas), and some others, such as dahlias, hellebores, anemones and wild flowers, benefit from having about 5 cm (2 in.) of the stem end dipped in boiling water for 30 seconds. The flower heads and leaves must be protected by being wrapped in a cloth. This is particularly suitable for rose buds limp at the neck. Afterwards give them the usual long drink.

Singeing: (q.v.) flower stems which exude milky latex when cut – poppies, spurge, poinsettias – need to be singed in an open flame (a candle is best) to seal them.

Floating: roses, hydrangeas and other wilted flowers respond to being floated on water for an hour or two. First recut the stem end.

Re-cutting stems under water: anyone trained in ikebana (q.v.) will do this for all stems, not just wilted ones. Have a bowl of water handy and re-cut the stem end *under* water, then give it a long drink.

Defoliating completely: lilac, philadelphus, laburnum need to be completely stripped of leaves so that enough water can reach the flower heads. Sprays of leaves can be arranged separately.

Aftercare

Water should be topped-up daily if possible. In the first ten or twelve hours plant material will, it is estimated, take up 75 per cent of the water it will need in the next two or three days.

A misting spray of water over flower heads and leaves during the 'long drink' stage and after arranging helps to reduce the loss of water through transpiration by keeping the atmosphere humid. Do this as often as you can in central heating or in very hot weather, but protect polished surfaces as you do so.

These preparations may seem something of a chore to the flower arranging newcomer, but they very soon become routine, and the time taken is assuredly well spent.

CONES, FLORIST

Florist's cones (or flower tubes) are like ice-cream cornets made of green plastic. Mounted on sticks they are used to hold one or more short-stemmed flowers to raise them higher in arrangements.

Wire or tape each one firmly to a garden cane or stick (*see* **MECHANICS** page 115), fill it with a little crumpled netting and make sure it can be topped up, as it does not hold much water. Cigar tubes or the little phials in which orchid or anthurium stems are packed can be used in the same way for a single flower. Flowers and foliage in the arrangement usually hide the cone and stick quite satisfactorily.

CONES, TREE

Coniferous trees provide the arranger with cones in various sizes and shapes which can be stored for years. The smallest come from the cupressus trees and shrubs and are greatly varied in themselves. They are used for collage or petite arrangements. Larch cones remain on graceful branches as the needles fall in autumn. Those with turned-out scales from the Japanese larch (*Larix kaemferi*) are prettier than the European species (*L. decidua*). Sequoia cones are segmented and unusual; cedars are barrel-shaped; firs are cylindrical with bracts to the scales; and the pine produces the most familiar wooden cones that are almost indestructible.

Cones need to be wired with false stems for use in arrangements.

Cones, Tree *Wiring a cone: push a stub wire between the lower scales and bring the two ends together to make a false stem. Finish off with stem binding tape.*

CONSERVATION

All flower arrangers should be aware of the need to conserve the natural heritage of plants, starting in their own and friends' gardens and learning to cut for arrangements with discretion and common sense. Here are elementary rules:

1 When cutting from a shrub or tree have regard for its natural shape and don't cut from just one side or indiscriminately.
2 Cut neatly to a bud or joint, with sharp cutters or a knife, leaving no unsightly snags.
3 Don't take all the leaves from bulb flowers as they are needed to make food for next year.

4 Leave some flower heads to seed, or to develop for autumn drying.
5 Consider planting a wild patch for birds, bees, or butterflies and moths. Wild plant seed is available from most seed firms.

On a wider scale flower arrangers can play a more active role in conserving (*a*) the countryside and wild plants and (*b*) cultivated plants and gardens by joining one of the local groups of the two main conservation organizations (*see* **APPENDIX: ADDRESSES** for the Royal Society for Nature Conservation and the National Council for the Conservation of Plants and Gardens).

CONTAINERS

Whereas at one time a container was simply a vase, a bowl, or occasionally a basket, today a flower arrangement container can literally be anything that does, or can be made to, hold water. For preserved, dried and artificial arrangements, even that requirement is not necessary.

To enumerate all the possibilities would be tedious but there are some guidelines that help. Most beginners try to use a container that is far too large and too deep for the available flowers. Very few arrangements for the average home need to be in a container more than about 15 cm (6 in.) in diameter unless it is a shallow dish or bowl for a landscape design or where some of the water is to show and be a significant feature.

Home-made containers such as painted tins or plastic bottles, string-covered cylinders, saucers or upturned flowerpots are just as acceptable as expensive antiques provided they suit the flowers, the setting and the occasion. It is suitability of size, shape, colour and style that counts, not expensive outlay. If someone's first reaction to an arrangement is 'what a beautiful/unusual/intricate/lovely coloured container that is', then the arrangement isn't doing its job.

Matt finishes are generally more useful than shiny ones, and white can be very dominant and eye-catching unless white flowers are being used.

Whilst virtually anything can be used as a container, arrangers acquire a basic range for their cupboard or shelf and for most people this will include:

Saucer or dish: ceramic or plastic, designed to take a round of floral foam.

Urn: ceramic or, more likely nowadays, plastic which can be painted or sprayed. Look for good proportions of the bowl to the stem and the base, whether it is sturdy or squat, or taller and more elegant.

Tall-stemmed container with a cupped top: perhaps supported by a cherub or other figure.

Tall cylinder: ceramic or home-made from a plastic bottle or tin. Ideal for more modern designs and may have more than one opening. Often needs weighting with sand or stones.

Basket: a shallow one with a relatively high handle is the easiest to start with. Fit it with a tin, plastic box or bowl or casserole dish to hold water. (*See* **BASKETS**)

Wide low dish: for 'water' arrangements, probably with well-pinholder to hold stems.

Bud vase: for a single bloom.

Candlestick (or bottle): for improvising a tall container by adding a candlecup.

Piece of chunky driftwood: with a cavity to hold a small container or well-pinholder for landscape designs, etc.

Several painted tins: use various sizes and shapes as unseen containers, e.g., baking, loaf, sardine, pie, baked beans, ham tins. Use matt paint or spray and choose colours such as black, grey, dark green or khaki which will blend in and be inconspicuous.
Add to these as opportunity or need arises.

If some containers tend to scratch tables, glue small pieces of felt on the contact points underneath.
Flower club sales' tables and local florists carry a selection of flower containers. If there is a local potter near you explore his/her stock, especially for modern, textured pots. *Flora* magazine, obtainable at newsagents and bookstalls has a good mail-order service. NAFAS leaflet No. 12 (*see* APPENDIX: ADDRESSES) gives instructions for a number of simple home-made containers.

CONTINENTAL STYLE
Sometimes also called the 'parallel' style, this has been dubbed the 'continental' style more recently, since it has its origins in Belgium, France, Germany, Holland and Italy.
These are the principal characteristics.
1 Stems do NOT radiate from one point but each stem has its own point of origin. This results in more or less parallel stems and lines which are mostly vertical, but can be horizontal or diagonal as well.
2 Flowers, foliage and any other components are used in blocks or zones of one kind, colour, shape or texture. Consequently, there is rarely a focal point and interest is distributed through the design.
3 The 'naturalistic' style, with plant material arranged as it would grow. The Italians' *linea rettangolo* (rectangular line) has been part of their repertoire for many years. One can create the effect of flowers, leaves and grasses growing in a field, ditch, hedgerow, woodland or garden.
4 More stylized versions have design-conscious horizontal/diagonal placements. Some are certainly modern/free-style, or even abstract, but the massed clusters and blocks of flowers, whilst not exactly traditional, do have their origins in the so-called 'western mass' style.
5 If horizontal placements are used, then blocks of floral foam must be large enough to contain the stems inserted sideways. They are often covered with sculptured or overlapping leaves and flowers, making another block within the overall design.

CONTRAST
Contrast is one of the **design principles** (q.v.). The word immediately suggests 'opposite' or 'different', and opposites are often needed to give interest to an arrangement with dark contrasted with light, rough with

smooth, vertical with horizontal and so on. But there are the subtler contrasts, too, which are part way towards complete opposites. Black and white may be the opposites, but grey being a mixture of the two provides the variation or half-way house. Transition and gradation can ease a sharp contrast (one extreme to the other) into a gentler one (variation). In traditional design that is often what is needed; sharp contrasts belong, in the main, to free-styles and abstracts.

Contrasts must obviously be considered with the other design principles: balance, rhythm and dominance in particular. Too much contrast, or too little, can affect them all.

CRAFT CLASSES

Certain classes in competitive shows are considered to be 'craft' classes as they cannot normally be created at the show and are therefore brought already assembled. They include collage, garland, mobile, picture, pressed flower picture, swag and such items as Christmas crackers, decorated parcels, decorative trees, etc.

At NAFAS national shows, and some others, these classes are *excluded* from consideration for the *Best in Show* award, on the grounds that it is unfair to compare something that has been created at leisure, at home, perhaps over a long period, with exhibits that have to be staged *in situ* with all the possible stresses and unforeseen problems.

CREATIVITY

The Americans use this word rather as the British use **originality** (q.v.). Esther Veramae Hame'l in her *Encyclopaedia of Judging and Exhibiting* (*see* **APPENDIX: BOOKS**) defines it as 'freshness of concept . . . creativity is imagination made visible . . . [it] distinguishes an art from a craft.'

Like originality, it is not easy to put into words, for there is nothing truly new under the sun, and one sympathizes with the judge who said, 'I can't describe it, but I shall know it when I see it.' Jean Taylor, at the beginning of her book *Creative Flower Arrangement*, refers to creativity as 'challenging the rules, trying out new methods, new techniques and new plant materials' and of 'experimenting continually to find out and learn . . . roving about with an enquiring mind . . . and absorbing ideas from the environment '

The creative arranger will not be one who is content to stay in a rut but one who seeks to create something, more beautiful, more rewarding, knowing he/she will have a thousand failures for perhaps one soul-satisfying success.

CRESCENT

One of the so-called **geometric styles** (q.v.), popular in the 1960s, at its most attractive when following the curves of the moon in the first or third quarters, with one side taller than the other, giving asymmetrical interest. When used 'reversed', like an upturned basin, the sides are usually equal. This way it is much used for table decoration in a tall-stemmed container, which is essential for the downward curves. The other essential is plant material with a natural curve to form the outline, and broom, willow, rosemary, forsythia and young budding branches are all useful for this purpose. Floral foam, coming well up above the container rim, is by far the easiest stem support to use.

DAY SCHOOLS or WORKSHOPS

Day schools organized by flower clubs or local education authorities normally concentrate on one aspect of flower arrangement or a closely allied craft. Practical work by the student is an essential feature. Preparation and organization by the tutor(s) need to be really detailed as the day is usually a 'one-off' and there is no opportunity to rectify deficiencies, no second chance, and no 'next lesson' to recap, consolidate or correct. It is essential for students to have a detailed brief well in advance and to do some homework for the day.

Good subjects for a day school include: abstract, Christmas, church flowers, collage, colour, period designs, pressed flower pictures, show work or table decorations. (*See* CLASSES)

DECOUPAGE

This art of decorating with paper cut-outs, derived its name from the French *découper*, to cut out. The Italians, *arte povero* imitated fine lacquer work; the Victorians padded their cut-outs and called the result *repoussé*; flower arrangers of the 1980s adopt a three-dimensional version by raising up parts of a picture.

Four identical pictures are needed for decoupage, and a complete one is glued to card, wood or a tile for the base. The main feature of the picture is then cut from its background in the second print. The cut paper edges are tinted, and the picture laid over the base, but raised up about 3 mm ($\frac{1}{8}$ in.) on blobs of silicone rubber sealant (sold for waterproofing joins in aquariums, kitchens or bathrooms). The third stage 'lifts' more important parts and these are contoured slightly by curving and modelling to give even greater depth. A final lift of some finer details completes the picture, which can be varnished or glazed and set in a deep frame.

Almost any picture can be tackled, but beginners should try a print with a clearly defined outline and not too much fine detail.

DEMONSTRATOR

A flower arranger who demonstrates the art of arranging at flower clubs or other meetings. Most are amateurs in that they do not make a living this way, but a number are professionals. Their programme usually lasts about one and a half hours and they will need at least an hour's preparation. They will be paid a fee plus travelling expenses and an agreed amount for flowers. These will almost certainly have to be augmented with foliage, etc. from their own or friends' gardens.

Most national flower arrangement organizations have some system of testing and accrediting demonstrators. NAFAS (q.v.) has a two-tier system whereby would-be demonstrators take a test which gives them 'area' status if they pass, and after three years, they can take a harder test to qualify as 'national' demonstrators.

DEPTH

The measurement given in show schedules to indicate the distance from front to back of the space allowed, e.g., 75 wide × 90 high × 65 cm deep or 30 × 36 × 27 in. It is also the factor which gives a third dimension to flower arrangement and so avoids a flat, cardboard-cut-out look. To increase the sense of depth:

1 Arrange plant material extending backward from the container – almost as far as that coming forward at the front.
2 Angle bases, and even containers, towards the diagonal of the space being used, leaving space at the back as well as at the front and sides.
3 Turn flowers to show their profiles and backs as well as full-face.
4 Leave space between flowers and leaves.
5 Recess some flowers and leaves so that all are not on the same plane.
6 Use advancing and receding colours, and light against dark or vice versa to 'lift' some colours from others.
7 Overlap some of the materials used in collages and pictures.
8 Use a container that is footed or stemmed, or a base raised on an unseen block to create shadows beneath and the illusion of greater depth.
9 Changes of texture from rough to smooth or matt to shiny, help to create depth.

DESICCANT

A drying agent which absorbs and holds moisture. Those most commonly used for drying plant materials are sand, borax and silica gel; sand may take weeks to dry a flower, silica gel a day or two. All desiccants need to be dried out before re-use. (*See* **DRYING** and **PRESERVING**)

DESIGN ELEMENTS

The elements of design are those qualities which every object possesses: form, line, colour and texture *plus* space.

Each of these attributes, shown in the diagrams of a hosta leaf on page 54, plays its part in any design, whether it is the interior decor of a room, the layout and planting of a garden, the creation of a fashion outfit or a flower arrangement. Consider the design qualities or elements of each piece of plant material and use them consciously and to advantage when applying the principles of design which are described below. (*See* **COLOUR, FORM, LINE, SPACE** and **TEXTURE**)

DESIGN PRINCIPLES

The design elements are tangible things; the design principles are concepts. Understood and thoughtfully applied, they can be a fine check list for any arranger who runs into difficulties with a design.

The principles are: balance, proportion, scale, rhythm, contrast, dominance and harmony (or unity). Some years ago one of my classes made up a useful mnemonic: 'big pink stones roll constantly down hill'.

Each one is dealt with separately under its alphabetical entry, but it is interesting to note here that if you examine what you think is a good flower arrangement, or any piece of designed work, then the arranger will probably have applied all the principles. If one principle has not been well used or ignored then total harmony or unity will not be perfect. How well the elements are used in carrying out the principles is what finally controls the excellence or otherwise of any created piece of work.

It is impossible to consider one principle of design without relating it to the others. Proportion is closely bound up with scale, contrast with dominance,

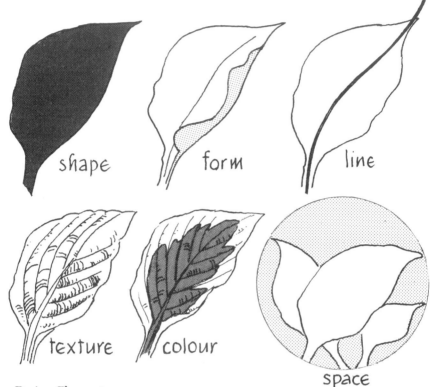

Design Elements

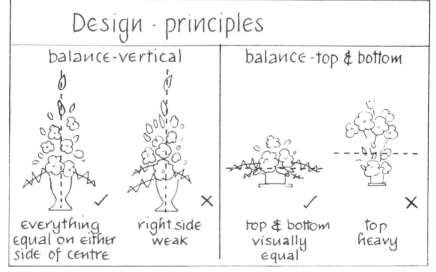

Design Principles *Some examples of how the design principles work.*

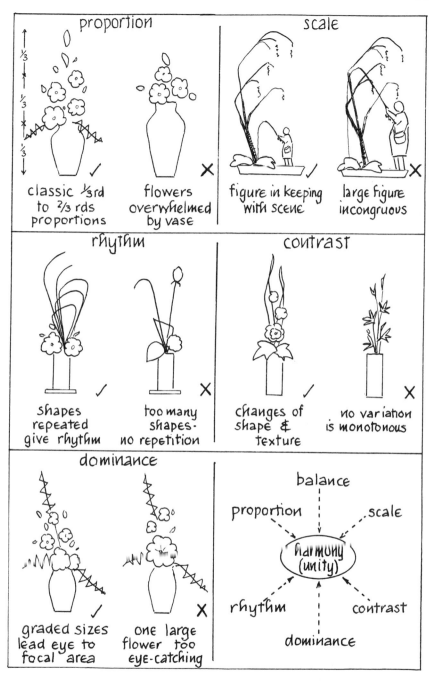

balance with rhythm and so on. Too much contrast, for example, can ruin balance, as is often seen in show exhibits interpreting 'contrasting' titles, such as *War and Peace* or *Summer and Winter*. Yet if the contrasts are balanced, then nothing is dominant, and interest is too evenly divided. It is the fine working together of all the principles that results in real harmony. (*See* BALANCE, CONTRAST, DOMINANCE, HARMONY, RHYTHM, PROPORTION and SCALE)

DESIGNER FLOWERS

The name was adopted in the later 1980s to describe the kind of arrangements so often seen in magazine photographs of interior decor or in window-dressing. Deceptively simple, but carefully thought out and placed as part of a 'roomscape', designer flowers add colour, texture or shape to a setting. As arrangements, their mechanics and execution may call for no great skill, but devising what to put where demands flair and a knowledge and understanding of design. Take a look at any interiors magazine and see how the flower arrangement is important not so much in itself, but as a vital ingredient of the whole room.

DISTINCTION

A word used in judging flower arrangement which rewards a quality of excellence or individuality which makes an exhibit outstanding.

DOMINANCE

Also called emphasis and one of the **design principles** (q.v.). One or more features dominate a design by reason of their size, quantity, shape, brightness of colour, shiny texture or position in the design at the top or in the foreground.

In competitive flower arrangement the plant material is expected to be the dominant feature, and all other parts of the exhibit should play a secondary, supporting role. All too often, one sees exhibits where the large container or accessory, the expanse of background colour or the piled-up bases have become dominant over the plant material; a judge will **down-point** (q.v.) for this. However, where flowers are used as part of an exhibition piece, or in the home or church, it is for the arranger, or perhaps the occasion, to decide what should be dominant. For example, at a flower festival in church, an arrangement by a statute or tomb should *not* be the dominant, but the complementary, feature.

Dominance is seen in traditional massed arrangements in the grouping of larger, brighter flowers and leaves toward the centre of the design. The eye needs a focal point or area, and good design leads the eye to these resting points. However, the focal points should not normally be so much of a bull's-eye that the rest of the arrangement has no visual attraction.

When two or more arrangements are featured as part of a design they should be unequal in height, size or colour attraction, and this will contribute to greater overall harmony.

DOWN-POINTING

A term that should strictly be used only in a judging system which has a specific number of points to award for a particular aspect, e.g., condition of plant material, composition, use of colour or interpretation.

It is, nevertheless, also used where points are not specifically awarded (as under NAFAS rules), and a judge 'mentally' down-points an exhibit for wilting plant material, lack of balance, untidy staging, ugly mechanics showing or something similar. In these circumstances it is essential that some scale of importance for the seriousness of the fault should be applied consistently. In this lies the art of a good judge.

DRAPE

Fabric used behind, underneath or in association with a show exhibit was very popular in the 1960s, especially draped from a point behind the centre of a symmetrical arrangement or from one corner of a niche behind an asymmetrical one. These drapes established a colourful setting and they helped to focus attention on the flowers.

With the advent of more free-style and abstract designs, draped fabric was seen to be old-fashioned and inappropriate, and the plain or pleated fabric panel or fabric-covered board and background became more popular. However, drapes are still seen in traditional designs and are useful to provide rhythmic linking between various items in large group displays. But it is easy to overdo the draping, and gardeners in particular deplore the use of too much fabric. Christopher Lloyd once referred to a NAFAS exhibit at Chelsea Flower Show as having a 'plethora of drapes'.

Types of fabric

Velvet has lost some of its popularity, probably because man-made jersey-type fabrics are far less expensive and drape more elegantly. Brushed nylon has an excellent matt finish and is available in many shades. Uncrushable material makes it much easier to get drapes to shows without creases, though it is still sensible to roll fabric on a cardboard tube for storage and transport. Avoid too pronounced a pattern with net, lace, brocade or tapestry used as a backing. Hessian/burlap will not drape and is better used as a panel.

Most jersey fabrics do not fray, but with any material that does, cut it with pinking shears or overstitch the cut edges. A hem makes it almost impossible to roll without marking. (See **BACKGROUNDS**)

DRIED WOOD/DRIFTWOOD

Most arrangers call any type of dried wood 'driftwood' and include bark, root, branches and stripped ivy in the term. Driftwood does not, however, include woody spathes and seedheads.

Driftwood is invaluable in landscape, freestyle and modern designs, and small pieces are useful to hide mechanics. Before use, make sure any dried wood has been:

- wire-brushed and all soft, rotten parts cut or scraped away, (brush greyed wood gently to preserve the attractive colour)
- thoroughly 'de-bugged' with disinfectant or 'Rentokil' if necessary
- trimmed to remove any awkward or ugly bits
- provided with a balancing 'leg' if needed (see **MECHANICS**) or trimmed to stand level and firm
- waxed or coloured IF NEEDED. Very often, this is not necessary, as the natural colouring blends well with all types of flowers and foliage, but shoe polish can be used to alter the colour slightly

Several different metal supports for fairly small pieces of wood can be purchased: a free-standing clamp with its own heavy base; one with an inverted pinholder to push down onto another pinholder; or a heavy base with a central screw about 3.5 cm ($1\frac{1}{2}$ in.) long (see **MECHANICS** page 116). Larger pieces can be screwed, more or less permanently, to a large base, or set in a mound of plaster of Paris or Polyfilla, painted to tone, to be free-standing.

DRYING AND PRESERVING

The good cook needs a store of well-chosen packet, tinned and frozen foods for use in emergencies and to supplement fresh supplies. The good flower arranger needs a store of plant material dried, pressed or preserved with

Driftwood *Driftwood and other preserved materials arranged by Maureen Gibson, Hassocks Flower Club, in a class 'Sculptural Beauty'.*

glycerine to help out in the lean winter days or to provide long-lasting decorations.

There are *four* different preserving processes: three of drying and one which replaces the water in plant material with a glycerine solution. The chart on pages 62–3 suggests which is most suitable for what.

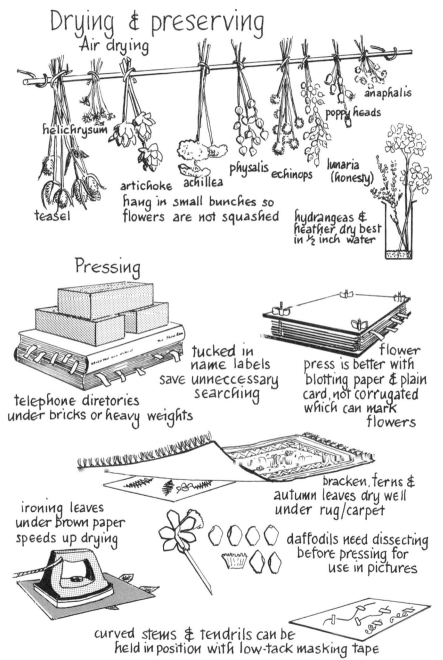

Drying & preserving
Air drying

anaphalis

poppy heads

helichrysum

artichoke achillea physalis echinops lunaria (honesty)

hang in small bunches so
flowers are not squashed

teasel

hydrangeas &
heather dry best
in ½ inch water

Pressing

tucked in
name labels
save unneccessary
searching

flower
press is better with
blotting paper & plain
card, not corrugated
which can mark
flowers

telephone diretories
under bricks or heavy weights

ironing leaves
under brown paper
speeds up drying

bracken, ferns &
autumn leaves dry well
under rug/carpet

daffodils need dissecting
before pressing for
use in pictures

curved stems & tendrils can be
held in position with low-tack masking tape

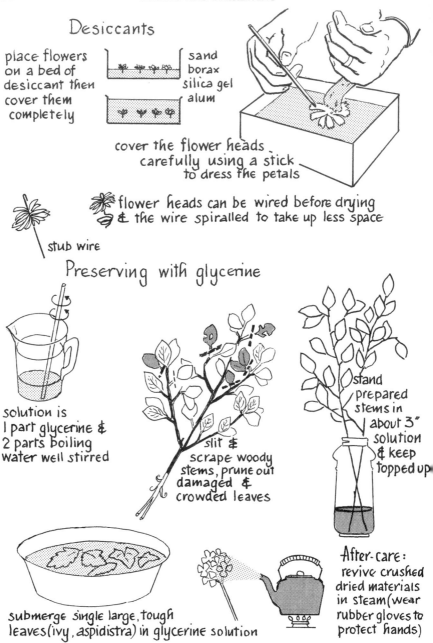

Desiccants

place flowers
on a bed of
desiccant then
cover them
completely

sand
borax
silica gel
alum

cover the flower heads
carefully using a stick
to dress the petals

flower heads can be wired before drying
& the wire spiralled to take up less space

stub wire

Preserving with glycerine

solution is
1 part glycerine &
2 parts boiling
water well stirred

slit &
scrape woody
stems, prune out
damaged &
crowded leaves

stand
prepared
stems in
about 3"
solution
& keep
topped up

submerge single large, tough
leaves (ivy, aspidistra) in glycerine solution

After-care:
revive crushed
dried materials
in steam (wear
rubber gloves to
protect hands)

Drying

There are a few golden rules; the rest is best learned from experience.

1 Gather plant materials to be dried at their peak of condition, and on a dry day, because flowers or leaves that are too damp tend to go mouldy quickly.

2 Select only well-formed, unblemished material; don't waste time on anything not in peak condition.

3 Pick only as much as you can handle in one session.

Air drying: This is most suitable for seedheads and 'everlasting' flowers which will in fact dry naturally on the plant, but will suffer rain and wind damage that way. Any leaves on the stems will shrivel, so should be removed before the stems are tied in loose, small bunches and hung upside down in a dry, airy place, preferably in the dark and certainly not in sunlight. A garage in summer, or a loft, is excellent. Arrange the bunches so that the flower heads come at different heights and do not crush each other.

Hydrangeas and heather are better dried standing upright in about 1 cm ($\frac{1}{2}$ in.) of water, which should not be replenished. Amaranthus (love-lies-bleeding) should also stand upright or the long tassels dry at an awkward angle.

Pressing: It is essential to lay out the plant material very carefully, and to cover it with equal care to avoid creases or curled edges in petals or leaves. These can seldom be corrected as dried plant material is very fragile.

Small flowers and leaves can be pressed between the pages of a thick book (old telephone directories are excellent) or in a special flower press, bought or made at home. The advantage of making your own press is that it can be the size you want and can have plain, stiff card rather than corrugated (which leaves stripes on flowers) between the layers of absorbent paper or blotting paper. When using books, lay heavy weights on top. In either case label the contents clearly to avoid too much shuffling about looking for what you need.

Larger single leaves can be pressed with a warm iron under a sheet of absorbent paper, to speed up the drying process. It is better not to use newspaper for this as the heat can transfer the printer's ink onto the leaves.

Large sprays of bracken, ferns and leaves can be spread between sheets of newspaper under the carpet or rugs. Try to avoid a place that gets a lot of heavy traffic.

Using a desiccant: This is a slightly trickier process, so start with something fairly small like little spring flowers or small roses. Because flowers that are desiccant-dried are very fragile, many arrangers prefer to wire flower heads first, cutting off most of the stem, then pushing a hooked stub wire down through the head. The wire can be coiled round to take up the minimum of space. Next choose a desiccant: sand, borax or silica gel.

Silica gel is perhaps the most popular today because it is quick, and few flowers will take more than four days to dry. It can be bought finely ground, specifically for drying flowers, or from the chemist as crystals, when it may need crushing with a rolling pin to make it finer. In either case, the silica gel must be *dry* (which means blue if tested with litmus paper) before use. If in doubt, dry it out spread on a baking tin in a very slow oven. When cool again, it is ready for use.

Plastic freezer boxes or ice cream containers are excellent to hold a number of smaller flowers. Put a layer of desiccant at the bottom, then carefully place the flowers on it. Very gently, sift desiccant over them, using a wooden skewer to 'dress' the petals and to make sure all the crevices are filled. When they are fully covered with about 2 cm ($\frac{3}{4}$ in.), put on the lid, then label the box with name of the flower or leaf, *and the date.* It is better to have just one kind in a box. Boxes should be looked at on the third day to assess progress, as, for the best results, it is important not to over-dry.

PRESERVING CHART

Method	Suitable material	Average time taken	Colour retention	Form
Air-drying	Seedheads and everlasting flowers	2–4 weeks	Good – better if done in the dark	Retained, but leaves shrivel
Pressing	Flowers and leaves that are not fleshy or bulky, separate petals, tendrils, thin stems	4 weeks	Very good	Flattened
Using a desiccant (borax, sand, silica gel)	Many-petalled or bulky flowers, grey leaves	2 weeks or more with sand or borax, 1–4 days with silica gel	Very good	Retained
Using glycerine	Leaves mainly, some seedheads, a few flowers	1–2 weeks, longer for some tough leaves	Changes to a tint or shade of brown, from cream to near-black	Retained and lasts for years

Examples

'Everlasting' flowers: acroclinum, achillea, amaranthus, anaphalis (pearly everlasting), gomphrena globosa (globe amaranth), helichrysum (strawflower), hydrangea, lavender, pampas grass, rhodanthe, statice

Seedheads: acanthus, allium, artichoke, bulrush, echinops (globe thistle), honesty, iris, nicandra, nigella (love-in-the-mist), physalis (Chinese lantern), poppy, salix (pussy willow), teasel

Flowers: buttercup, celandine, crocosmia, daisy, freesia, forget-me-not, grasses, hellebores, honeysuckle (lonicera), larkspur, mimosa, pansies, primroses, Queen Anne's lace

Petals: rose, daffodil (cut trumpet in two), potentilla

Leaves: autumn-coloured acer, beech, etc. Bracken, bramble, cupressus, ferns, grey leaves, raspberry

Stems: buttercup, primrose

Tendrils: sweetpea, clematis, vine

Leaves: grey and silver

Flowers: auricula, carnation, clematis, daffodil, dahlia, hellebore, hollyhock, larkspur, narcissus and many more

Leaves: (single or sprays) aspidistra, beech, box, broom, camellia, choisya, cotoneaster, cupressus, fatsia, ferns, garrya, ivy, laurel, magnolia, mahonia, oak, rhododendron, polygonatum (Solomon's seal), whitebeam

Flowers/bracts: alchemilla, hydrangea, sea holly, lime tree, molucella (bells of Ireland)

Seedheads: antirrhinum, dock, foxglove, teasel

Catkins: garrya, salix (pussy willow)

Borax is the lightest in weight of the desiccants and suitable for very fine and delicate flowers. It tends to adhere to the dried petals and is not always easy to brush off. For this reason it is often mixed with sand, either roughly half and half or two parts of sand to one of borax.

Prepare boxes as for silica gel, but expect that drying will take up to four weeks, or longer for thick and fleshy petals.

Sand has been used for centuries to dry flowers. It is the heaviest desiccant and slowest-acting, but for that reason, timing is less crucial and flowers seldom over-dry in sand. Silver sand (from horticultural suppliers) seldom needs cleaning. Industrial sand needs to be washed through and thoroughly dried out in a warm oven before being used with flowers. Once clean it will not need to be rewashed, but must be dried out between each use.

Use in the same way as other desiccants.

Preserving with glycerine

Contrary to the drying processes, preservation with glycerine involves the replacement of water in the plant tissues by glycerine, which preserves their form but changes their colour. The process is most suited to leaves. All leaves, flowers and seedheads treated with glycerine turn brown, but the colour varies from a pale biscuit to virtually black. The colour can usually be lightened, after preservation, by standing leaves in a sunny window or conservatory.

The solution: Mix one part glycerine with two parts boiling water, preferably in a glass jar where the solution level can be seen. Anti-freeze liquid may be used instead, but then a 1:1 solution is preferred. A depth of about 8 cm (3 in.) is sufficient for stems to stand in, but it must be kept topped up, so that they do not dry out.

Prepare the stems or branches as for **conditioning** (q.v.) by cutting on a slant, slitting and scraping if woody, and by cutting out damaged and crowded leaves. Glycerine today is not cheap and it is a waste to preserve leaves that will be discarded before arranging. They take up unnecessary room as well.

Within a short time, a darkening colour will spread out from the veins in leaves; when the whole leaf or spray has changed colour, the preservation is complete. Remove stems from the solution. In theory, the solution can be used again, but even after re-heating it, I have not found this satisfactory.

Single, tough-textured leaves such as ivy, fatsia and aspidistra can be submerged in the glycerine solution in a shallow container. To keep the leaves fully submerged, cover with a cloth soaked in the solution.

Storage: Dried and glycerine-treated materials are better stored separately. Polythene tends to encourage damp and mildew and preserved material is better in cardboard boxes with tissue or newspaper between layers when necessary. Keep the boxes in a dry place (not in cold damp sheds or garages in winter) and check fairly frequently to be sure mice and insects aren't feasting on the harvest.

Re-furbishing: After a while preserved materials get crumpled or flattened. Revive them by holding flower heads and sprays of leaves in the steam of a boiling kettle, shaking and shaping them as you do so – remember to wear rubber gloves. Stems can be curved, if necessary, into more pleasing lines when softened.

If glycerined material has become really dusty in use, or mildewed, swish it through warm soapy water, then rinse in clean water and allow it to dry thoroughly before putting it in store. (*See* **SKELETONIZING** *and colour section*)

DUTCH/FLEMISH (c.1600–1800)

Holland, in the seventeenth century, was a wealthy maritime power, trading and colonizing all over the world, and especially in the Far East. Rich middle-class merchants prospered from the making of delftware, fine linens and velvets and dealing in precious metals. Their love of gardens and flowers could be enjoyed even during the long gloomy Dutch winters with the vivid floral paintings they hung indoors. It is astonishing that such a huge number of flower-pieces should have been produced in such a comparatively short period by painters from so small a country. Their strict Calvinist religion and belief in the brevity of man's life and the sin of indulging in the pleasures of the senses seems very much at odds with the riotous, abandoned, colourful vases of flowers which have come to be known as the Dutch/Flemish style. They never existed, in fact; they were paintings composed from notebook studies. The simple little vase of glass of flowers seen in some paintings of interiors on mantelpieces, tables or window ledges, is probably nearer to reality.

typical domestic style

'vanitas' objects

flowers in a glass jug with a gilt rim

Delft tulip vase

flowers in a terracotta vase & fruit (after Jan van Huijsum)

Dutch/Flemish *Features of the Dutch/Flemish style (1600–1800).*

Settings
Buildings with stepped gables were of brick faced with stone, and shuttered windows of small rectangular panes of glass; interiors were simple with black and white, or black and terracotta chequered floors; hangings of velvet silk or linen often fringed; white table cloths; Delft tiles; pewter and sturdy glass tableware.

Colours
Cool muted interiors; much black, grey and white in costume; hangings of dark brown, dark green, deep blue or crimson with gold fringe. Flower arrangements were polychromatic and almost luminous.

Flowers and plants
The tulip, especially if striped or streaked, is virtually synonymous with seventeenth-century Holland when tulipomania swept the country and fortunes were spent on bulbs. The tulip appears in almost every Dutch flower-piece, but so too do anemone, auricula, carnation, crown imperial, hollyhock, iris, lily, poppy, narcissus, rose, snowball flower and vivid blue 'morning glories'. There is little foliage other than that on the flower stems, but poppy and vine leaves are featured. All kinds of fruit were used including apricots, cherries, corn ears, gourds, grapes, lemons (usually cut with the peel curling over the edge of the plate or table), melons (often with a wedge cut out to show the inner flesh), nuts, oranges, peaches, pears, pineapples, plums and pomegranates.

Containers
Blue and white delftware dishes and bowls, squat metal or terracotta urns, knobbed glass tumblers, clear glass carafe or decanter shapes and sometimes low baskets.

Bases
Stone and marble ledges, plinths, wooden tables.

Arrangements
The style gradually changed from rather stiff little bouquets in the early seventeenth century, to gentler curves and downward flowing lines with rather more flowers, and in the eighteenth century the paintings of Bosschaert, Van Huysum, Van Brussel and Van Os show an exuberant profusion of curving stems and petals in lush abundance. Flowers are turned in every direction with large and important flowers at the top. S-curves sweep through the composition, and the light glows on paler flowers.

Accessories
They have a special significance in this period and are known as 'vanitas' (vanity) to remind man of his earthly sins and inevitable death – insects, reptiles, snails, guttering candles, watches, hour-glasses and skulls. But there is always a ray of hope in the bird's nest with eggs and butterflies symbolizing the soul.
(*See* PERIOD ARRANGING)

EDWARDIAN (1900–1914)

The first part of the twentieth century in Britain, after Queen Victoria's death, was bound to be influenced by the **Art Nouveau** decorative style (q.v.) and by some revolt against the over-cluttered Victorian style. The Edwardian style was less formal and more elegant and the period is often referred to as the Long Summer and the last age of elegance. There were two sides, as always, to the coin. The well-to-do lived enviable lives with motor cars, telephones, theatre and sport, but the Trade Union and suffragette movements focussed attention on the poverty of the working classes.

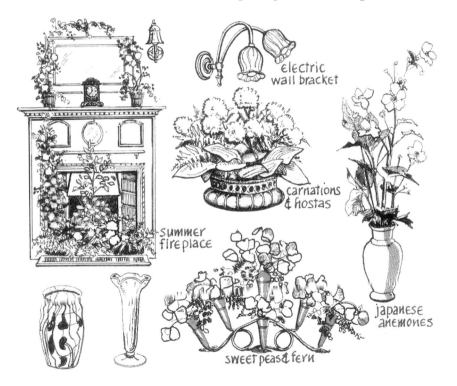

Edwardian *Features of Edwardian arranging (1900–1914).*

Settings

Furniture was less heavy and decorated and rooms less cluttered; simpler lines were seen everywhere; fireplaces lost the heavy overmantles; woodwork was painted matt white; stained glass panels were seen in windows and doors; lighter woods such as satinwood, ash and light oak were popular; fringed lampshades decorated the 'new' electric light fittings; and silverplate was a status symbol if you could not afford real silver.

Colours
These were less garish than in the previous century with subtler tones of cream, lilac, pearl-grey, turquoise and grey-green with tasteful colour harmonies. The iridescent hues of mother-of-pearl, butterfly and dragonfly wings and peacock feathers were popular.

Plant material
Carnations and sweet peas are probably most typical, but chrysanthemums, too, make an entry, with dahlias and orchids. Lilies, lilies of the valley, roses (especially the 'cabbage' types) and peonies continued in favour with gypsophila for lighter, lacy effects. Simple bunches of Parma violets were worn or carried. Fruit blossom was used and forced.

Asparagus, smilax and other ferns were much used, also beech (both green and copper), coloured leaves from indoor and conservatory plants, vines, honesty (*Lunaria annua*) seedheads (to accord with the mother-of-pearl look), pampas grass and Chinese lanterns (*Physalis alkekengi*).

Containers
Tall glass vases in trumpet and other shapes, especially cut glass and the coloured and metallic finishes popular with Art Nouveau designers; epergnes with silver-plated stands and small glass, fluted-edge trumpets; shells; Indian brassware vases and bowls; copper and pewter jugs and bowls and ceramic basket shapes.

Arrangements
For the most part, arrangements were simple hand bunches, often of one kind of flower, placed in vases, but with a lighter, more open look than in Victorian times. The influence of Japanese ikebana was being felt, and low bowls with water arrangements of iris or daffodils were quite a vogue. Dining-tables for grand social occasions were still elaborate and often fanciful, but gradually the emphasis on 'tasteful' became paramount.

Accessories
Whilst none appears specifically associated with flowers, any Edwardian ornament or *objet d'art* could be used to create period atmosphere, especially flowing draperies of georgette, silk or gauze, peacock and ostrich feathers, mother-of-pearl or butterfly wing ornaments, jet beads and parasols.

Symbolism
The interest in the 'Language of Flowers' of Victorian times abated gradually and the outbreak of World War I in 1914 terminated the Long Summer. (*See* **PERIOD ARRANGING**)

EGYPTIAN, ANCIENT (c.3000–323 BC)
An advanced civilization which flourished in the narrow fertile valley of the Nile. An ordered, little-changing society, the first with a national government, it produced hieroglyphic writing and highly skilled architects, metal workers, sculptors, painters and other craftsmen. Life was a preparation for death and eternal after-life, so elaborate tombs were built for the Egyptian rulers, the Pharaohs. From the excavation of these (notably that of Tutankhamun) we have much information about their lives, skills and beliefs.

Settings
Monumental palaces, tombs, temples and pyramids with huge pillars and statues; elegant furniture and artefacts; gold (silver was rare), alabaster,

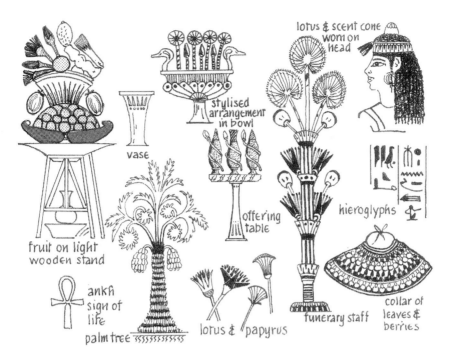

Egyptian *Designs from Ancient Egypt (c.3000–323 BC).*

ivory, faience; gardens provided shade and water for coolness and irrigation; tomb paintings in flat areas of bright clear colours, with no shading but stylized outlines of human figures and faces; pleated white and unbleached linen and lawn, imported silks.

Colours
Terracotta red, green, darker blue and turquoise, yellow, white, black and gold.

Flowers and plants
The lotus (*Nymphaea caerula*) – the blue water-lily sacred to Isis, goddess of the Nile – is featured prolifically in tomb paintings and artefacts, both as decorative motifs and as flowers used for social occasions and ceremonies; papyrus (*Cyperus papyrus*), an aquatic plant used to make paper from strips woven into mats, and the love-apple (*Mandragora officinarum*) are the plants seen most frequently; berries, cornflowers, willow, olive and palm leaves were used for collarettes and garlands; blue iris, anemone, narcissus, mimosa, violet, mignonette, doum palm, vines, lettuce, ivy, olives, pomegranates, dates, figs, grapes, melons, onions and gourds were also prolific.

Containers
Lotus vases with several spout openings, stemmed bowls, tall vases wide at the top decorated with gilt, semi-precious stones and paste.

Bases
Flat rush baskets, offering tables and light wooden stands.

Arrangements and uses
Lotus was worn in chaplets or as a single flower on the forehead, often with perfume cones placed on top of the head that gradually melted to release scent. Lotus stems, or bunches, were hung over shoulders and arms, curved round jars, carried in metal or wicker pokes, arranged in many-spouted vases, or laid over offerings. Collarettes were decorated with leaves, beads, flowers and slices of love-apple. Lotus was arranged in bowls in stiff symmetrical pattern of twos or threes, with buds. Papyrus, lotuses and love-apple were used in tall (up to 2 metres (6 ft)) funerary staffs, again in twos or threes. Garlands for ceremonial purposes with leaves, flowers and berries. (*See* **PERIOD ARRANGING**)

EQUIPMENT, *see* **TOOLS**

EXHIBIT

Under NAFAS rules/phraseology all *show* entries are referred to as 'exhibits', superseding the old descriptions 'arrangement' (meaning without any accessories), 'composition' and 'design' (both of which allowed accessories). This is fine, since an 'exhibit' can include accessories or not as the competitor wishes. What is not so good is the tendency for show-conscious newcomers to be afraid to use the old terms for anything, even skirting round the very word embodied in the NAFAS name, 'arrangement'. This becomes absurd when one is complemented on one's *exhibit* on the piano, sideboard or bedside table – or worse still, on the altar in church!

Flower arrangements are still 'arrangements' at home, in church, in the library or hospital. Design is perhaps a good word to use for free-style and abstract concoctions, and display or exhibition pieces for larger presentations, but let's leave exhibits where they belong – in competitive shows. (*See* **SCHEDULES, SCHEDULE DEFINITIONS, SHOWS**)

FABERGÉ, CARL (1846–1920)

Carl Fabergé, skilled goldsmith, became jeweller to the Tsars of Russia, making for them a series of superb Easter eggs in metals with precious stones and enamels, which command a fortune today. He also made exquisite jewelled flowers and animals, decorated boxes and brooches. His work has been an inspiration to nimble-fingered arrangers who enjoy handicrafts, and led to a great interest in egg-decorating and the creating of 'Fabergé' fruits and boxes, painted or fabric-covered and decorated with gold and silver braids, cords, sequins, beads, pearl-headed pins, plastic leaves and flowers and stones from fake jewellery.

FIGURINE

Figurines of china, glass, wood, metal or plaster have long been popular as accessories to flower arrangements both at home and in shows; birds and animals add interest to landscape scenes and madonnas to Christmas designs. Hand-made figurines from hessian, paper sculpture or Polyfilla-soaked cloth (which sets hard) are suitable for certain designs, and the three crafts have a number of adherents.

There are several helpful hints to remember when using a figurine:

1 Scale is of the utmost importance. In a show exhibit the figurine should not be dominant because of its size, colour or shiny finish. A reasonable guide is that the figurine should not be more than two-thirds the height of the arrangement, but, in contrast, if it is too small it may look ridiculous.

2 If two or more figurines are used in a design they must be in scale with each other.

3 The size of the largest plant material used is important too. A large gerbera, dahlia or rose can dwarf a delicately-modelled figurine.

4 The style and surface texture of the figurine should be in keeping with the style of the arrangement. A sleek, stylized figure will look curious in a naturalistic landscape, or a dainty crinolined lady with chunky driftwood and chrysanthemums.

5 Try to pick up and echo the line, form, colour or texture of the figurine in the plant material.

6 A base on which both arrangement and figurine can stand helps to unify the whole picture.

(*See* ACCESSORY)

FILMS, *see* VIDEOS

FLEUR-DE-LIS

The heraldic lily, emblem of the royal house of France, is generally thought to be based on the iris flower, not the lily. Shakespeare called it the 'flower-de-luce'. In the 1960s the fleur-de-lis shape enjoyed a limited vogue as a style of flower arrangement, especially for pedestal work. The waisted outline was more economical of plant material than the more conventional solid triangle shape.

FLOATING ARRANGEMENT

Classes for children or adults at local village/horticultural shows sometimes include a floating arrangement. Flower heads and leaves are floated in a low bowl and there seem to be two styles: one, a closely packed geometric pattern, often multicoloured and in concentric circles; the other, a looser asymmetrical design with naturalistic curves and carefully thought-out colour scheme. The floating arrangement was popular in the 1920s and '30s when flower heads were floated round a bird figurine in low bowls of yellow, orange or blue outside and black inside.

It is important that any water area left showing should be clean and free from bits. The shallower the water, the more easily a loose design will hold.

FLORAL ARTIST

A title favoured by some countries, e.g., South Africa, New Zealand and America rather than **flower arranger** (q.v.). To British ears it sounds rather pretentious. The floral artist may be male or female, professional or amateur.

FLORAL FOAM

Green
The substance that changed the mechanics of flower arranging! A man-made, green, spongy foam (from about 1970 on) which absorbs and holds water, and stems at any angle. Popularly called **Oasis** (q.v.), the trade name for the best-known brand, but similar foams sell under other trademarks such as Bloomfix, Flora-foam, etc. Oasis is now available in three grades: *economy* – a lighter weight foam for smaller or temporary arrangements; *ideal* – general purpose; *premium* – for large arrangements and the heaviest stems.

Brown
The brown or fawn, crunchier-textured foam does *not* hold water and is intended for dried, preserved and artificial stems.

Both types are available in blocks about $23 \times 11 \times 8$ cm ($9 \times 4\frac{1}{2} \times 3$ in.), in cylinders (or rounds) about 8 cm (3 in.) diameter and 5 cm (2 in.) deep and in cones, spheres, wreath rings, trays, posy holders and other shapes.

Tips for use
1 Cut the green foam to size or shape needed while still dry to avoid waste (though it can be cut wet).
2 Allow the foam to sink into a bowl or bucket of water by its own weight. Water will then soak right through the block. This will take only a few minutes. When almost completely submerged it is ready for use.
3 The block needs anchoring into a container: (*a*) with a pronged holder fixed to the base; or (*b*) with tape crossed over it and stuck to the container; or (*c*) with a cap of 2 cm ($\frac{3}{4}$ in.) mesh wired over it and secured round the container.

4 The foam must protrude above the top of the container by at least 2 cm ($\frac{3}{4}$ in.) for a small arrangement and up to 8 cm (3 in.) for a larger one, so that stems can be pushed into the sides as well as the top.

5 Wrapping the foam in thin dry cleaners' polythene helps to reduce water evaporation if daily watering is not possible or difficult.

6 When a piece of foam has been used once, turn it over in the container before using it again. Two, or sometimes three, uses are possible if care is taken and the block is not honeycombed by many stems.

7 If pre-soaked foam is to be stored, it must not be allowed to dry out, but kept damp in a sealed plastic bag.

8 Be sure to use the sides as well as the top when inserting stems. Push them in only just far enough to hold firmly, to avoid honey-combing the block.

9 Dry foam needs to be anchored just as securely and should be used in the same way as the green (tips 1, 3, 4, 6 and 8).

(*See* **MECHANICS** for diagrams, *also* **TOOLS and EQUIPMENT**)

FLORAL SCULPTURE

The term crept into use during the late 1970s and early 1980s to describe constructions and assemblages, usually inspired by and created from plant materials (and therefore done by flower arrangers), though other items such as shells, perspex, metal, found objects and throwaway junk were incorporated. They are usually classed as abstract flower arrangements.

Large-scale floral sculpture has great possibilities for exhibition display pieces in halls, theatres, office blocks and hotels, but its execution often requires a supporting cast of carpenter, welder, engineer and architect! It is an aspect hardly explored, and on this scale perhaps beyond the scope of the amateur. (*See* **ABSTRACT**)

FLORIST/FLORISTRY

In the seventeenth and eighteenth centuries in Britain, the florist was a skilful gardener and plant hybridist who, in his backyard garden bred the florist's flowers: anemones, carnations, hyacinths, pinks, polyanthus, ranunculi, tulips and, later, pansies.

The florist as a seller of cut flowers and houseplants, and maker of bouquets, head-dresses and wreaths is a more recent connotation. As a retailer of *artificial* flowers, the description is more recent still.

Generally speaking, the florist today is the professional owning or working in a retail shop, and the flower arranger is the amateur. A florist will be trained to wire and make up bouquets, bridal flowers and funeral tributes and to handle the commercial side of ordering and buying at the market and organizing the shop. He/she needs to be deft and able to work under pressure to complete orders by a certain time.

The availability of floral foams has done much to reduce the need for florists to wire all plant materials, but the skill is still needed. Experience in a shop is expected of students taking the City and Guilds floristry examinations. The highest qualification in professional floristry in Britain is the National Diploma of the Society of Floristry. (*See* **APPENDIX: ADDRESSES**)

FLOWER

Botanically, the flower is the reproductive part of the plant from which the fruit or seed develops. It is also (usually) the most colourful part of the plant and frequently its greatest beauty.

The term flower includes both single blooms (tulip), blossom (forsythia), catkins (hazel), flowering grasses, coloured bracts (hydrangea), sedges and rushes (bulrush or reedmace) and cereals.

FLOWER ARRANGEMENT

A misleading term; floral art is more accurate, but thought to be pretentious. The flower arranger uses all kinds of plant materials including leaves, stems, fruits, vegetables, cones, seedheads, lichen, moss, wood, fungi and cereals as well as flowers. Usually, materials are cut from their parent plant, but growing plants are used in **pot-et-fleur** (q.v.) for example, and can be included in any arrangement.

The flower arrangements themselves may include many styles and methods from the simple bunch popped into a vase to the elaborate church pedestal; Christmas door wreaths, swags and garlands; the tiny miniature in a thimble; pressed flower picture; planted bowl or construction of driftwood and contorted reeds. To say, as many do, that some of these things are not 'flower arranging' is taking a blinkered view. It may not be pretty and one may not personally like it, but creating something with plant material is the essence of the arranger's craft. Carried to its highest pinnacle of achievement it *is* floral art.

Because of the wide variety of styles of arrangement, there can be no rules for setting about the task, but some guidelines may be helpful:

1 Avoid using too large a container. It dwarfs the flowers and often makes it difficult to cover up mechanics.

2 Don't feel that time spent on conditioning and preparing the mechanics is wasted. It never is.

3 Don't cut flowers that are already wide open and past their peak. That is a waste of time. Indoors they will quickly shrivel or shatter, whereas left in the garden, there may be several days still to enjoy them.

4 Try to avoid having any two stems of exactly the same length on the same level. Attention is drawn to anything that begins to look like a line, and is held there.

5 *Three* is a useful number to remember:
(*a*) three flowers are always easier to compose than two or four.
(*b*) even a bowl or vase of one type of flower is more interesting with three different shapes – buds, open flowers and leaves.
(*c*) modern or freestyle designs seldom need more than three different types of plant material.
(*d*) work in threes when building up a traditional design whether symmetrical or asymmetrical: three tall stems to form the backbone; three at each side, three towards the front, three towards the back to give depth; three larger leaves and three larger flowers at the focal area.
(*e*) proportions of three to two (*see* **GOLDEN SECTION**) are usually pleasing. Get into the habit of thinking in thirds.
(*f*) use more than three accessories only with the greatest discretion.

FLOWER ARRANGER

While some flower arrangers do earn money from teaching, demonstrating or arranging flowers for special occasions and events, they are, for the most part, amateurs enjoying a hobby, and often helping to raise large sums for charities through shows, festivals and exhibitions. The flower arranging 'movement', as it is often called, blossomed after the Second World War and now has thousands of adherents world-wide – 100,000 in Britain alone. (*See* **FLORAL ARTIST**)

FLOWER CLUBS

Known variously as flower arrangement societies, floral art groups, flower decoration guilds, flower and garden lovers' clubs and many variations on this theme, flower clubs comprise groups of people (mostly women but the number of men members is growing) who meet, usually once a month, to practise and enjoy the art of flower arranging. Most have been formed since the mid-1950s and by 1988 there were 1,400 clubs in Britain and overseas affiliated to NAFAS alone. Many clubs were originally formed by and from horticultural societies and many still stage joint shows each year.

Club membership varies from as few as 15 in rural areas to 500 in a city. Meetings usually include a demonstration of flower arrangement by a visiting expert or a talk on an allied subject. Members can buy flower arranging equipment and accessories from sales tables, borrow books from the club library, order magazines and other publications, hear about all the local and national events and book tickets for them. Day schools, courses of lessons, visits to shows and gardens are also organized. Over the years the emphasis has gradually changed from members learning how to arrange flowers themselves, to watching demonstrations by others as an entertainment.

FLOWER FESTIVALS

Flower festivals are usually held in churches or stately homes. The chosen building is decorated not as it would be in every day use, but as a spectacle to attract visitors, to raise money or to celebrate a special event. Such festivals commonly last two or three days, sometimes a week.

Organization

The organization of a festival, large or small, is best undertaken by an *ad hoc* committee, each member having a specific area of responsibility such as design, publicity, printing, finance, stewards and so on. For a large festival the organization may start a year before the event.

A clear division of responsibility between the festival committee and the owners/trustees of the building must be made at the outset and the monies to fund the undertaking fully agreed. This, and responsibility for publicizing the event, are the two most likely areas of uncertainty and misunderstanding and must be clearly defined and agreed in writing early on. It is important that *one* person, usually the chairman of the organizing committee, should be the contact between the house owners or church authorities and the organizing committee. It saves a deal of overlapping, confusion and irritation.

One person, or a team of, say, three, should be given the task of planning the whole design and deciding the place, size, colour and style of each arrangement or display. Arrangers can then be invited to take part. They may be drawn from local groups associated with the church or house, or from a wider area of the diocese or county, and even nationally and internationally for festivals at major cathedrals organized by a national association. A viewing day (or two) must be organized for the arrangers to come and see the venue, discuss their allocated task and consult with the designer(s) about problems. This viewing day is essential so that arrangers can absorb the atmosphere of the house or church, see the actual colours in the setting, and the light, take accurate measurements, make sketches and perhaps take photographs. Whether arrangers are expected to finance their own display or will receive full or part payment must be agreed before going further.

Staging and dismantling

The organizing committee must give accurate instructions on staging and dismantling times, unloading, car parking, arrangements for water supply, topping up, disposal of rubbish, storage space or work-rooms, covering of precious floors or furniture, loan of containers or stands, refreshments, exhibitors badges and so on. If something special or unusual is expected of an arranger or group, the designer(s) should be prepared to attend and approve a mock up. The gap between what a designer hopes for and describes, and what is perceived by the arrangers, may be a wide one and everything possible should be done to bridge it.

Publicity

Publicity, more than anything else, makes or mars the financial success of festivals, yet is so often left in the hands of a volunteer who hardly knows the ropes. If possible enlist the aid of someone with press or public relations experience and work out a complete campaign in good time. The 'lead' time for publishing advertisements, articles and so on is always longer than you think. Personal contact is worth a thousand press handouts.

Tickets, handbills, posters, brochures and programmes all play a part in publicity but may have to be handled by another committee member who must liaise closely.

Stewards, guides and helpers

The organization, time-tabling and *briefing* of stewards and helpers will take all one committee member's time, persuasiveness, commonsense and not a little tact.

FLOWER PICTURES

Pictures made from dried flowers and leaves are a type of collage and may be flat or three-dimensional, depending on whether the materials are all pressed, or still retain their form after air or desiccant drying.

Pressed flower pictures

For pressing techniques *see* DRYING. To make a picture it is often sensible to choose the frame first and design the picture to go with it. Pressed plant materials are delicate and subtle in colour, and too heavy a frame can be overwhelming.

Use a rigid board for the background (hardboard, Daler board or thick cardboard are suitable) and paint or cover it with fabric or paper as wished. Avoid a heavily textured surface. Handling the pressed material as little as possible and using tweezers and a flat knife, try out the design. When it seems satisfactory, lift each piece carefully and stick it down with one or two spots of a latex or clear glue applied with a cocktail stick. Pictures should be glazed to prevent curling and non-reflecting glass gets rid of confusing highlights. Seal the back of the picture to prevent dust and condensation. Colours do fade over time, but less quickly if the picture is out of direct sunlight. Greetings cards, calendars and gift tags will be made on thinner card or heavy paper and for protection can be covered with adhesive clear plastic or a fine gauze or chiffon stretched over and glued to the back.

Three-dimensional pictures
These are made in a similar manner, and sometimes pressed flowers and leaves are used for the outline, with the three-dimensional flowers built up from them. If framed, a deep box-frame will be needed.

Animal, bird and scenic pictures
Dried plant materials are used to create other types of pictures, both flat and three-dimensional. Shape, colour and texture can emulate birds' feathers, fish scales, butterfly wings or features in a landscape.

Artificial colouring, frowned on by purists, can be done with water colour paints or water-soluble felt-tipped pens.
(*See* **FRAMES**)

FOAM ANCHOR/HOLDER
Variously called an anchor, holder, frog or prong it may be in metal with a heavy lead base and five to seven long but widely spaced pins, or a small cheap plastic four-pronged gadget. Both are effective to secure a block of floral foam, though the plastic holder is really only suitable for an arrangement under 30 cm (12 in.) high. Fix either kind to the container with putty-type adhesive such as Oasis-fix. (*See* **MECHANICS**)

FOLIAGE
Foliage (meaning 'leaves or leafage'), and its use in arrangements, is said to differentiate the amateur arranger from the commercial florist. The amateur, often a gardener, usually has access to a far greater variety of foliage than can be bought in the markets. The recent trend towards planting more shrubs than herbaccous plants, to cut down on the work in the garden, strengthens this argument.

Whilst the term 'foliage-arranger' is an unlikely one, so-called flower arangers often make arrangements of leaves with no flowers, but very rarely indeed of flowers with no leaves.

The temperate climate in Britain gives a variety of foliage rarely enjoyed by any other country – variety in leaf shape, colour and texture. Even in winter, evergreens (and there are ever-yellows and ever-greys as well) provide a surprising range. The new arranger, even with only a small garden, will find it worth while to grow some favourite and reliable foliage.
1 Take note of the interesting foliage used by demonstrators. Their plants and shrubs have to stand continual cutting and long journeys in all kinds of weather, so are likely to be comparatively care-free. Cuttings may be available at demonstrations.
2 Remember that the variegated version of any plant will be slower growing than the plain green equivalent and perhaps suit the smaller garden.

Foliage *Spring foliage, hellebore flowers and mahonia berries show a variety of shapes and tones.*

3 Be patient. A plant/shrub needs several years to become established and big enough to cut from.

4 Look out for plants which will give you double, or even treble value. Whilst grown primarily for their fresh leaves, many will provide flowers or berries as well – e.g., hostas will give elegant flowers and black seeds for seed collage; arums, bright orange berries when established; garrya, catkins; *Viburnum tinus*, lacy flowers all winter; senecio, silver sprays of buds in summer and holly and skimmia, red berries. Almost all evergreens can be preserved with glycerine as well.

5 Before use, foliage, especially evergreens, may need washing. Swish branches through soapy water, then rinse in clear water. Shiny evergreens look well-groomed if wiped over with a pad dipped in oil. They should never look oily, but have a sheen like well-brushed hair.

There is no scope here to do more than suggest a short list of the shrubs and herbaceous plants worth considering both for interest in the garden and for cutting and lasting well indoors. The following are not really fussy as to soil or situation:

Herbaceous

Arum	*A. italicum pictum* is the marbled one, but all are useful.
Bergenia	*B. cordifolia* has the better shaped leaf. Hybrids like 'Silberlicht' and 'Abendglut' often turn to red-bronze in winter.
Ferns	There are many, all with difficult names. Most are useful. They prefer shade.
Hellebores	Apart from delightful apple-green flowers in spring, *H. corsicus* and *H. foetidus* have good evergreen leaves.
Hostas	The range is very wide today. Grow any of them, preferably in some shade and protect against slugs and snails, their chief enemies.

Shrubs

Aucuba	The spotted laurel is *A. japonica*. 'Crotonoides' has more gold mottling than most.
Choisya	*C. ternata*, the Mexican orange, has aromatic glossy green leaves and white flowers several times a year.
Cupressus	The range of colour and size is extensive. Beware of choosing one too large for your garden. The tough but feathery leaves are a fine contrast to shiny evergreens and may be green, grey, yellow or bluish, some with variegation.
Elaeagnus	*E. pungens* 'Maculata' and 'Limelight', with gold splashed leaves, are the ones to grow.
Holly	Ilex is the botanical name. 'Silver Queen' and 'Golden King' are worth growing. They take years to become full trees.
Ivy	Hedera comes in an infinite variety of shapes, sizes and markings and all are of value. Even when a severe winter cuts them back they leaf again in spring.
Mahonia	*M. aquifolium*, and *M. japonica* are the most usual ones. *M. bealei* leaves are yellow-green underneath and 'Charity' is bolder. Mahonia preserves well with glycerine.
Privet	*Ligustrum ovalifolium* 'Aureo-marginatum' is the forbidding name of the familiar golden privet which grows so easily and will withstand constant cutting, which is why it is so often clipped into a hedge.
Senecio	The hardiest of the grey-leaved shrubs with a white underside to the leaf. Variously called *S. greyii* or *S. laxifolius* in nurseries.
Skimmia	*S. japonica* is a female form with paler leaves than 'Foremanii'. Both have persistent red berries, and 'Foremanii' is said to be self-fertile.

(*See* **OIL** *and* **PLANT MATERIAL** *and colour section*)

FORCING BLOSSOM

In late winter and early spring almost all blossom can be forced into early flower if you cut it and bring it into the warmth of the house. It is an attractive way of speeding up the spring. Cut branches when they are in fat bud and arrange in warm water to start with, preferably in a deep jug or vase rather than in floral foam. Stand in good light, otherwise the colour may be very pale indeed. Worth trying are:

Aesculus hippocastanum	– horse chestnut
Chaenomeles	– quince
Forsythia	
Malus	– apple and crab apple
Prunus	– almond, cherry, plum
Ribes	– flowering currant
Salix caprea	– pussy willow

FORM

Form, the three-dimensional version of shape, is one of the **design elements** (q.v.). Since almost all flower arrangement is three-dimensional anyway (except pressed flower collage), the arranger, unlike the painter, has no need to create the illusion of form.

Rounded forms focus the attention and in design terms are known as 'points' (which is confusing to many arrangers). They may be regular, as in a perfect sphere or cube, or irregular, but they form a resting 'point' for the eye in any design including a flower arrangement.

More elongated forms, conical or rectangular, lead the eye in some direction towards something else. They help to create the movement and rhythm in a design, but are less obviously rhythmical than a line – which is another, closely related, element of design.

Volumetric form is one which contains space such as a cup, a bell or a lily flower.

FRAMES

The arranger will be concerned with the choice of a frame either for a pressed flower picture or a collage, whether of seeds or a mixture of pressed and three-dimensional plant materials. Take care in choosing both the width of the moulding and its style and colour so that it does not overwhelm the plant material.

Frames can be ready-made, ordered made to size, or, more economically, the cut lengths of moulding can be ordered and the frame assembled at home. With present day, fast-acting glues this is quite a simple job. The mitred corner cuts should be spread with a fast-setting epoxy-resin glue like Araldite Rapid. Assemble the frame on a flat surface using a right-angled set square to get accurate corners. Tie string right round the frame and use a stick as a tourniquet to ensure it holds the joints together tightly. Re-check the corner angles and leave to set. With small pictures it is not usually necessary to pin the corners as well, but a staple gun can be used to strengthen each join on the back.

Pressed flower pictures
These should normally be glazed for protection and the glass should press firmly and evenly over the whole picture to prevent curling. The choice of glass will depend on personal taste and where the picture is to hang. Clear glass often confuses the viewer with light reflections, but non-reflecting glass can give a slightly hazy look. The back should be well sealed with paper or plastic tape to make it dustproof.

Collages
There is always some degree of depth in a collage and if it is very three-dimensional, a boxed frame will be needed.

If you wish to make your own frames entirely, then invest in a mitre block and tenon saw. The mitres must be accurate or the result looks very amateurish.

FREE-STYLE

Flower arrangers seem uncertain what to call arrangements that are obviously not traditional masses but are in keeping with the simpler lines and bolder forms and patterns of modern architecture, sculpture, and furniture. At various times, and in various countries, these designs – and they are very design-conscious – have been described as *free-style, free-form, free-line, mass-line, modern* and *contemporary*. They all mean much the same thing in that they describe a style which has made the bridge from traditional to abstract flower arrangement. It is no easier to say precisely where the one begins and the other ends, than it is to define the point where red becomes orange.
    One can describe them as flower arrangements which:

● use far less plant material
● consciously use space as an integral part of the design
● are uncluttered and bold
● have irregular outlines
● generally emphasize asymmetrical balance rather than symmetry, and thus show the influence of **ikebana** (q.v.), which is always asymmetrical
● still use plant materials in a relatively natural way, though some manipulation for design purposes shows in looped pliable branches, bent stalks and clipped leaves
● use containers that are bold and simple in outline with an interesting texture and little added decoration

Designing free-style arrangements
Students used to massed arrangements who are at a loss how to start, could try the following:
1 Select a tall cylindrical container or a simple low bowl.
2 Secure a pinholder for the mechanics.
3 Use not more than *seven* pieces of plant material of not more than three different types, e.g., three branches, two leaves and two flowers.
4 By playing around with these pieces construct a design that is pleasing to your eye, keeping in mind the design principles, so that it is balanced but not symmetrical, has rhythm and some contrast of form, colour or texture yet makes a harmonious whole. (*See **picture overleaf and colour section***)

FRUIT

Although colourful, varied, long lasting, edible (so therefore economical) and needing no water supply, fruit is surprisingly little used by arrangers in Britain. Many fruits are inexpensive, but grapes are used most frequently and they are one of the most expensive! The term fruit normally includes vegetables, berries, nuts, cones, fungi and seedheads. Under NAFAS rules, it also includes catkins, cereals, reedmace, rushes, reeds, sedges and heads of grass at any stage of development. (*See* MECHANICS *and colour section*)

Colour	Round	Oval, triangular	Long and sprays
Red	apple, cherry, peach, tomato, radish, head of skimmia berries	pepper, strawberry	rhubarb, crab apples, rose hips, cotoneaster, hawthorn and holly berries
Orange	apricot, orange, peach, loquat, squash	pineapple, carrot, *Arum italicum* berries, bunches of sorbus berries	berries of pyracantha and *Iris foetidissima*
Yellow	apple, gourd, melon, grapefruit	lemon, pepper	banana, berries of pyracantha, holly
Green	apple, fig, gage, gourd, melon, cabbage, Brussels sprout, Kiwifruit (sliced)	pepper, lime, pear, avocado, bunch grapes	asparagus, peas in pod, runner bean, courgette, cucumber, unripe fruit/berries
Purple	damson, plum, sloe, bullace	aubergine, plum, bunch grapes	*Leycesteria formosa*
Black	Head of ivy berries	privet and hypericum berries	blackberries
Brown	hazelnut, walnut, lichee, onion, mushroom	cones, Kiwifruit, pear, potato, brazil nut	sprays larch cones
White	gourd, turnip, broccoli, button mushroom		parsnip, celery, leek, snowberries, wild clematis seedheads

Free-style Edith Brack's tall free-style design uses interesting shapes and textures.

Fruit *Fruit and foliage with a garden statue for a buffet table decoration.*

FUNGUS

Fungi such as mushrooms or some toadstools like the fly agaric (*Amanita muscari*) can be used in landscape arrangements. Bracket fungi will dry well and are used both in woodland designs or free-style, where they can often cover mechanics, because they tone well with wood and modern hand-thrown pottery. Use cocktail sticks (toothpicks) to anchor them. Bracket fungi need to dry out very gradually in a warm place such as an airing cupboard or over a central-heating boiler.

GARLANDS

Garlands are one of the oldest forms of flower decoration. The earliest known are those found in Tutankhamun's tomb in Egypt dating from about 1350 BC. Garlands of willow and olive leaves, blue lotus flowers and berries were placed on the king's coffin and hung round the necks of statues. Men and women of Ancient Greece and Rome wore garlands on festival days and honoured their gods and heroes with them. Renaissance paintings show garlands or **swags** (q.v.) of fruit, leaves and flowers, and the ceramic wreaths of Della Robbia are well-known. As late as the end of the fifteenth century in London churchwarden's accounts tell of priests wearing 'crown garlands' of roses and woodruff on St Barnabas' Day in mid-June. Churches in Greece are still decorated with ivy garlands for special festivals, and the custom of crown garlands is perpetuated by brides and bridesmaids. Evergreen garlands are still popular at Christmas time, and flower arrangers use them for festivals in churches and stately homes. There are two main methods for constructing long flexible garlands (see **MECHANICS**):

1 Using rope, washing line or the legs of nylon tights or stockings knotted together as the base, snippets of evergreens and flowers are bound on in bunches with wire or green twine. The stems and binding of one bunch are hidden by the next. If the greenery is well-conditioned before making up and the garland is mist-sprayed, it lasts a long time. Dried or preserved leaves, cones and seedheads will need wire stems before being used in this way.

2 'Sausages' of pieces of floral foam about $12 \times 5 \times 8$ cm ($4\frac{1}{2} \times 2 \times 3$ in.) wrapped in thin dry cleaners' polythene, with reel wire twisted between each block, are more manageable if encased in a tube of 2 cm ($\frac{3}{4}$ in.) wire netting. Twist the cut ends of netting on top if the garland is to be decorated on only three sides. Insert short pieces of foliage, wired cones, berries or flowers as wished

For circular garlands see **WREATH**.

GEOMETRIC SHAPES

Although the geometric shapes so popular in the 1950s and '60s are still used today and will continue to be used for a long while to come, their rather precise application to flower arrangement already seems dated, and they are much looser in style than they were.

At the time of their popularity, however, many people were being attracted to the newly-forming flower clubs, all avid to learn the art and craft of flower arrangement. Teachers were comparatively few, and they and the writers of books and magazine articles needed some framework on which to base their instruction. Diagrams, geometric in outline, were soon dubbed triangular, crescent-shaped and so on and provided help, ideas and a common language for newcomers to the art. As so often happens, what were

Garlands *A garlanded bust and column for a NAFAS flower festival at Woburn Abbey. Arrangers: Peggy Crooks and Kay Wallington.*

intended as guidelines came to be taken as rules, and were often rigidly applied. The categories include:

curved – crescent, reversed crescent, Hogarth curve, oval, circle and spiral; *straight* – L-shape, vertical, horizontal, diagonal, zigzag and the triangles, both symmetrical and asymmetrical.

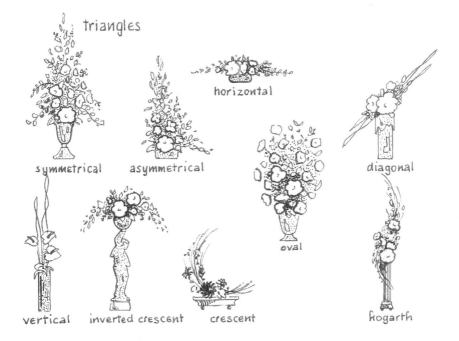

As with traditional massed arrangements, in each of the geometric shapes there is a gradual transition from fine plant material making the outline and the larger, rounder shapes at the central focal point.

The triangular shape has remained by far the most popular in Britain and continues to be considered the ideal outline for pedestal arrangements and formal massed designs. There is good reason for this, as the broad base given visual stability and there is movement and rhythm as the eye moves towards the pointed tips. Over the years the proportions have altered somewhat, in that a taller triangle is now considered more elegant than the squat triangular arrangement of the 1960s.

GEORGIAN (1714-1830)

The Georgian period, the 'Age of Elegance', coincides roughly with the eighteenth century, but extends through the Regency (1811-1820) to the end of the reign of George IV in 1830. A prosperous era (in spite of the effects of the French Revolution in 1789 and the loss of Britain's American colonies) it produced superb artists, architects, cabinet-makers, silversmiths, potters and makers of porcelain. It was fashionable to 'take the waters' at the spas, to frequent coffee houses, and to do the 'Grand Tour' if one was wealthy enough. Georgian design was eclectic, taking the best from classical, Chinese, Indian and Egyptian styles. The Brighton Pavilion displays this to the full.

Settings
Elegance and good proportions are seen in the best of domestic architecture, usually brick with stone facings and tall sash windows; furniture in the Chippendale, Sheraton or Hepplewhite styles; interiors with designs fully integrated by one designer (e.g., **Robert Adam**, q.v.); tapestries with scenes of classical mythology; chinoiserie; classical pillars; gilt mirrors; and damasks, silks and 'toile de Jouy' (a heavy printed cotton).

Colours
In decor grey-green and blue, rusty-pink and soft browns were favoured, with white painted wood and plasterwork; in clothes and furnishings, Chinese yellow, turquoise, peach, clear red and dark green were popular, but colour combinations were never gaudy. Carved decorations, whether in wood or plaster, were often gilded. Flower arrangements were polychromatic, but not garish, and some one-colour groups began to be seen.

Plant material
The variety of flowers was extensive, many grown in hot-houses and special cutting gardens because of the fashion for garden landscaping without flowers. 'Quality' flowers are typical: rose, lily, carnation, peony, lilac, tuberose (*Polianthes tuberosa*), iris, delphinium and antirrhinum. The tulip was still popular, and the auricula was one of the 'florist flowers' being specially bred and shown in little staged 'theatres' or display stands. Robert Furber's *Twelve months of Flowers*, 1730, often seen in reproduction prints, records a whole range of available flowers.

The 'everlastings' dried for winter decoration were strawflowers (helichrysum), globe amaranth (gomphrena) and pearly everlasting (anaphalis). Not much additional foliage was used. Fruit to grace the dinner tables included pineapples, oranges, melons, lemons, peaches, apricots, figs and nectarines grown in orangeries and hot-houses, as well as the English orchard and soft fruits.

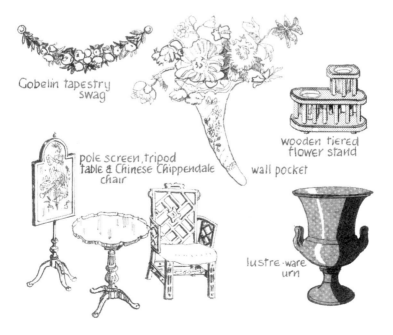

Gobelin tapestry swag

pole screen, tripod table & Chinese Chippendale chair

wooden tiered flower stand

wall pocket

lustre-ware urn

Containers

A wealth of containers was available in silver, pottery and porcelain: urns of all kinds, flower bricks with perforated tops, tall baskets with high handles, bough-pots, wall vases (or 'pockets' as they were called), shell-shaped bowls, five-fingered posy holders, Wedgwood, Rockingham, Chelsea, Bow, Derby and Staffordshire and Chinese export porcelain.

Arrangements

Most were symmetrical, either rounded or triangular. Colours were mainly polychromatic, some one-colour arrangements. Small vases, bough-pots of flowers, blossom and leaves in fireplaces in summer; urns, simply arranged on side tables and mantelpieces, wall 'pockets' of fresh flowers and dried arrangements were used in winter. (*See* **PERIOD ARRANGING**)

GIBBONS, GRINLING (1648–1721)

Gibbons was a woodcarver of genius, born in Rotterdam, but of English parents, who came to be Master Carver in Wood to King Charles II after the Restoration. He worked from nature, mainly in lime wood, which he laminated in two or three layers; he also used box, oak and pear wood for low relief work. Flowers, fruits and leaves, with birds, cherubs, and ribbons are woven into superb swags and garlands. Some are gilded; most are in their natural wood colour.

The wheel comes full circle when Gibbons' work is used as inspiration for the flower arranger, who emulates the elegant carved profusion with actual dried and preserved plant materials.

His work may be seen at Petworth House, Lyme Park, St Paul's Cathedral, Hampton Court Palace and many London city churches.

GLYCERINE

Glycerine in a solution of one part glycerine to two parts hot water, is used to preserve leaves and seedheads for almost indefinite use in arranging. Anti-freeze, sold for car radiators, may be used instead, though it is usually more effective as a 1:1 solution. (*See* **DRYING**)

GOLDEN SECTION/MEAN

Sometimes also called the Golden Number or Golden Ratio, the term describes an irrational proportion, thought for centuries, and at least since the time of Euclid, to be in hidden harmony with the proportions of the universe. Loosely stated the ideal division of a line is in the proportion one-third to two-thirds, or more precisely in five parts to eight parts.

Designers, artists and flower arrangers find these proportions easier for the eye to accept as harmonious than something divided in half.

GREEK (600–146 BC) and ROMAN (AD 28–325)

These two periods are generally considered together, so far as flower arrangement is concerned, because they had much in common: their Mediterranean climate and plants, love of outdoor activities, architecture and sculpture and even their gods. During their colonization of Western Europe the Romans brought gardening to Britain.

Greek vases

flower patterned mosaic

thrysus

mosaic basket

wall painting at Pompeii

Ionic column

Greek and Roman *The two ancient civilizations of Greece (600–146 BC) and Rome (AD 28–325) have many characteristics in common.*

Settings
Columns in the classical orders; coloured marbles of white, green, yellow, black and purple; brilliantly painted interiors; colourful painted statues; Roman courtyard gardens ('peristyle'); Roman pictorial and black and white mosaic floors; acanthus leaf decoration; temples in olive and citrus groves; amphitheatres.

Colours
Rich terracotta red, black, dark green and golden beige for interiors; fabrics in saffron (for brides), Tyrrhenian purple (for emperors), red, emerald and apple green; flowers in mixed bright colours.

Plant materials
The rose was the flower of Rome; Athens was the 'violet-crowned city'. Also used in garlands were anemone, asphodel, cornflower, honeysuckle, hyacinth, iris, lily, narcissus, poppy and tulip. The Mediterranean shrubs, trees and herbs were used for strewing and garlands: bay, box, cupressus, ivy, myrtle, oak, oleander, rosemary and vine. Fruits such as cherry, grape, lemon, melon, medlar, olive, orange, peach, pear, plum and pomegranate were used with vegetables, herbs and berries.

Containers
It is not thought that flowers were much arranged in containers. They were certainly collected, and may have been arranged, in baskets – both low ones and tall beaker shapes. The 'cornucopia' or 'horn of plenty' holds flowers, fruit and leaves in some decorations.

Flowers and their uses

Essentially, plant materials were used, not in containers as we understand them, but as garlands, chaplets, circlets, wreaths and strewn as whole flowers or petals. They were gathered in baskets and carried (by the Romans, at least) in flower-filled scarves held across the body rather like an apron. Garland-makers were the florists of those times. Garlands were worn on the head, round the neck or over one shoulder and across the chest and hung to decorate temples and houses. The heavy be-ribboned swag of fruits and foliage, often seen in carving, was the 'encarpa'. Emperors wore chaplets of leaves, either real or wrought in gold, tied at the back with ribbons. **Strewing flowers** (q.v.) and petals was commonplace at festivals and processions or over guests at meals. The 'thyrsus', a tall slim staff carried especially at festivals of Dionysus/Bacchus was twined with ivy (the antidote for drunkenness) and topped with a pine cone, known as the 'pine-apple', with which the wine was flavoured.

Two actual examples of 'arrangements' are the mosaic from the Quintilii Villa of the second century AD, showing a basket of roses, carnations, hyacinths, anemones, narcissus and a tulip; and a fifth century BC Greek decoration showing women putting leafy branches (possibly myrtle) into tall vases, perhaps as part of wedding preparations.

Symbolism

Almost all uses of flowers and foliage were ritualistic. Floral offerings were made to their gods, either to plead with or to placate them, and each god had his or her own associated plant. The wreath or circlet was a symbol of eternity.
(*See* **PERIOD ARRANGING**)

GROUP EXHIBITS, *see* **LARGE-SCALE EXHIBITS**

HAND (OR TIED) BUNCH

A hand bunch is made up (usually by a florist) ready to be placed in a container of water without the need to untie or re-arrange the flowers.

Far more popular on the continent than in Britain, hand bunches are intended for presentation to a guest, a hostess or an important person. Nothing is wired and, although the effect is simple, such a bunch is not easy to assemble without practice. As the name implies, it is assembled in one hand, one stem at a time, with all the stems pivoting on the tying point. The bunch is tied with raffia or string, or bound with stem-binding (never with wire), and finished with a bow. Stems are trimmed level.

HARMONY

Harmony, also called unity, is one of the **design principles** (q.v.). In flower arrangement, as in any other designed work, whether it is painting, sculpture or interior decor, harmony is achieved by good use of all the other design principles and elements of form, line, colour, texture and space.

But true harmony, for a flower arrangement, lies in something more. It should be also in keeping with its setting, both in colouring and style, and be suitable for its function, whether that is to decorate a dining table or a church, cheer a hospital patient or put welcome on a door at Christmas time. John Donne's phrase, 'no man is an island, entire of itself', applies equally to a flower arrangement. It is part of its setting, and part of what goes on in that setting, and to be effective it must harmonize.

HOGARTH CURVE

A curve and reversed curve like the letter S (sometimes called the 'lazy S') named after **William Hogarth** (q.v.). It is one of the so-called **geometric shapes** (q.v.) of flower arrangement, but at its best is far removed from strict geometry.

It can be in the vertical plane or horizontal for a table decoration. If vertical, you will need a tall container and curved plant material for the outline, e.g., broom, rosemary, salix. For good proportions the top curve is rather longer than the lower one, and for good balance the focal point or larger plant material is more or less central to the line. Floral foam makes the best mechanics, but beware of having too large a piece which, when covered, makes the centre far too bulky for the outline.

HOGARTH, WILLIAM (1697–1764)

Eighteenth-century artist and engraver. In 1753 he published his *Analysis of Beauty* and referred to the S-shaped curve as the 'line of beauty'. He used this curve as the 'g' in his signature. Flower arrangers use the curve as an outline for arrangements.

HOLLOW STEMS

According to all flower arrangement manuals hollow stems should be filled with water before arranging, either with a syringe or a long-spouted can, and plugged with cotton wool. In twenty years of flower arranging I have never succeeded in doing this, so I won't recommend it!

HOME, FLOWERS IN THE

Most people arrange flowers in their own home more often than in any other setting. The flowers should always be more than an arrangement done in isolation and put down on any horizontal surface. They look so much better if arranged for their setting, which in turn, will be enhanced by the flowers. From time to time take stock of your home, your containers and, if you have a garden, what you grow in it that is available for cutting.

Style: is the house/room cottagey, streamlined modern, Victorian, formal, avant-garde?

Home, Flowers in the *A pedestal, a dried arrangement and a bowl of flowers with the family photos enhance the crowded, Victorian look.*

Colour and pattern: which are the predominant colours of the walls, carpet, curtains, upholstery and wood? Are they plain, floral, striped?

Where the flowers normally stand: most rooms have only comparatively few places where there is space. What shape is the space? Tall and narrow, wide but not high, L-shaped?

Light and aspect: does the room face north, south, east or west? Do nearby trees, buildings or water affect the daylight? Is the artificial light household tungsten or fluorescent strip? Is it central, on walls, up-lighters or free-standing shaded lamps?

Containers: what have you got? Which ones are the favourites? What have you always wanted?

Garden: if you have a garden to cut from, however small, consider growing flowers and shrubs that will suit your colour schemes and your style. It is surprising how often arrangers will grow, say, red tulips when their colour scheme indoors would look better with pink. If you would find a yellow cupressus more useful, why grow a dark green one?

Some thought and planning for your flowers in the home can lift them from merely pleasing to downright satisfying.
(*See* **TABLE DECORATIONS** *and colour section*)

HORIZONTAL
Another of the **geometric shapes** (q.v.), most popular as a long, low **table decoration** (q.v.).

HOSPITAL FLOWERS
Flowers for hospital patients should ideally be:

- ready-arranged – a patient confined to bed is unable to do her own flowers without asking the help of busy staff
- fairly small – there is little room on a locker or bed-table for large displays
- easy to move for meals, bed-making and ward cleaning – a handled basket is ideal, or a broad based low plastic bowl, but avoid tall, cockly containers
- well-conditioned, if fresh – hospitals are very warm. Long-lasting flowers and foliage are the best value, but a patient may love to have fragile short-lived spring flowers
- disposable, to save extra work – use a cheap container, plastic foam anchor (no expensive pinholders) or foam taped in
- pretty and cheerful but not too hectic in colouring

A dried arrangement does not have quite the same feel of the open air from which the patient is temporarily cut off, but may be appropriate in winter. Long-stay patients who are mobile may enjoy being taken a complete pack, to make their own arrangements, of container, floral foam, anchor or tape, flowers and foliage. Make sure scissors or cutters are available. Beware of very strong scents; they can be distressing, even unpleasant, to people who are ill. Many flower clubs have a regular rota for arranging flowers in hospitals, perhaps in the entrance foyer, the chapel or in wards. Anyone who has ever done this will know what interest and pleasure it creates among staff, patients and visitors. Flowers arranged in this way can be larger and more showy, but must never be in the way or cause problems to the daily work of the hospital. Use a container large enough to hold plenty of water. Take a large plastic sheet to work on; pack up rubbish (and take it home with you if disposal is difficult); clean and clear sinks; take your own dustpan and brush if none is readily available; and leave everything immaculate. Be sure to check whether you should top up water and tend the arrangement(s) for the week or whether it is someone else's specific task.

HOUSE PLANTS

The range of house plants today is extensive and many plant-lovers will enjoy them for their own sake.

House plants can be grown to provide some cut foliage for flat-dwellers who have no garden. Ivies (hederas) seem to thrive on cutting, and many of the quick-growing climbers do not resent it. For special use one may grow sansevieria, *Begonia rex*, maidenhair fern (adiantum), croton (codiaeum), zebrina, tradescantia or *Monstera deliciosa* – the Swiss cheese plant – to name but a few.

Use them in **pot-et-fleur** (q.v.) too. Plants grouped in a container as an arrangement are more attractive than a lot of separate pots in saucers.

IKEBANA

Ikebana, or Japanese flower arrangement, is more than a decorative art, it is also a spiritual discipline. The word means 'living flowers' or 'creating with flowers'.

When Buddhism spread to Japan from China in the sixth century AD, with it came the custom of offering flowers to Buddha. So at first ikebana was more of a temple art, then an aristocratic pastime, and during the eighteenth century it began to be practised by ordinary men. It was not until the middle of the nineteenth century that women took up ikebana. Today, there are many different schools with their own styles and rules. The best known in the West are Ichiyo, Ohara and Sogetsu.

All ikebana is asymmetrical, symbolizing the balance of opposites, and space plays an important part. Compared with massed western-style arrangements, ikebana uses great restraint and limited plant material. There are three symbolic main lines:

Shin, the longest line, represents Heaven;
Soe, the middle line, is Man;
Hikae, the shortest, stands for the Earth.

These main lines are of prescribed lengths in relation to each other and are placed at special angles from the vertical: Shin at 10°, Soe at 45° and Hikae at 75°. Basic arrangements in ikebana are always shown with a bird's-eye-view diagram as well as one viewed from the front, so that the correct *depth* of an arrangement is understood.

The three main 'styles' of ikebana are:

Rikka – very large formal arrangements which represent natural scenery
Nageire – which uses a tall cylindrical container
Moribana – which uses a wide, shallow bowl or dish

There are ikebana Chapters or Groups in many countries today all over the world, including several in Britain. Details from Ikebana International Headquarters in Tokyo (*see* **APPENDIX: ADDRESSES**).

IKEBANA INTERNATIONAL

Ikebana International was founded in 1956 by Ellen Gordon Allen, an American. The headquarters is in Tokyo and the motto, 'Friendship through flowers'. It aims to promote the study and spread of ikebana and a better understanding between peoples of the world. It publishes a magazine and newsletter and arranges tours by the Grand Masters throughout the world. Every five years there is a convention in Tokyo.
(*See* **APPENDIX: ADDRESSES**)

IMMERSING LEAVES, *see* **CONDITIONING**

Ikebana *Wood and hydrangeas for a non-competitive ikebana exhibit at a NAFAS festival.*

INTERFLORA

Interflora, the best known world-wide flower delivery service, was formed in
1923. Orders for flowers are telephoned to a member florist nearest the
recipient, so that fresh flowers can be delivered without delay. Today there
are some 45,000 Interflora florists in over 130 countries. Their symbol is
Mercury, the winged messenger of the gods. (*See* **APPENDIX: ADDRESSES**)

INTERPRETATION

Most flower arrangements for the home, office or church are purely
decorative, but in about 1950 arrangements began to appear in shows
which were interpretative of the title of the show or class. So although flower
symbolism (q.v.) is ages old, interpretation in flower arrangement is new
and of the latter part of the twentieth century. Its advent confirmed flower
arrangers as artists who might have something to say to their viewers other
than, 'look how pretty these flowers are'. It made them take a more
thoughtful look at all plant material and its qualities so that they could use
this medium to: * portray a landscape; * tell a story; * capture a mood; *
suggest a concept; * or comment on life or society.

Interpretation *Good design and interpretation do not date. Worthing Flower
Club's prize-winning exhibit 'Summertime' in 1968 stands the test of time.*

This, in turn, has led to almost all classes in shows having a title to be
interpreted. Some titles are easy, like 'The year's at the spring', 'Autumn
glory' or 'Lovely leaves', but others are more difficult, such as 'Pantomime',
'Odyssey' or 'Turbulence', requiring some research. There is also great scope
for interpretative arranging in church festivals when there are themes,
hymns, or bible texts to portray; in flower festivals at stately homes when

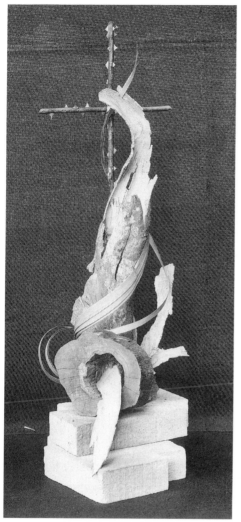

Interpretation *Dorothy Woolley's striking free-style design interpreting the building of Coventry Cathedral.*

historical events or features of the architecture or decor need to be depicted· and for other special exhibitions.

Although interpretative arrangements often tend to rely far too much on the use of **accessories** (q.v.), it is the plant material that should be telling the story. It can do this by the use of any of the following:

Colour: the greatest impact-maker, very emotive and usually the first thing to be thought of. *See* **COLOUR** for ideas of what each colour can convey.

Form/shape: the three-dimensional form of flowers can help in interpretation, e.g., bell-shapes, spheres, triangular leaves, chunky driftwood and cylindrical stems.

Line: stiff, straight stems, graceful curves, twisted tangles and pointed blade shapes can each establish a definite concept.

Texture: shiny, smooth, ribbed, hairy, gnarled, matt, velvety or rough textures each suggest a different quality (*See* **TEXTURE**).

Association: old symbolisms and emblems add their message, already understood by the viewer: red rose for love, lily for purity, poppy for sleep or the First World War, maple leaf for Canada, etc.

Although plant materials must play the star part in any interpretation, the supporting cast which may include container, base, background or drape, accessories and even a title or name, should play its part also. The style of the arrangement, too, should be chosen to enhance the interpretation. If the title suggests movement and activity then a static, massed triangle will not help to convey the idea, nor will an elegant line design suggest Victorian clutter.

Six steps in interpretation

1 Do some homework with a dictionary or thesaurus and perhaps a book of quotations to understand the title fully, however simple it is. Ideas are often sparked off by explanations and associated words.
2 Translate ideas into plant material, choosing colour, form, line, texture and perhaps association, carefully.
3 Assemble other possible items including accessories, choosing again for colour, form, line, texture or associations.
4 Having collected all this, select the best, try out in mock-ups, and reject all the rest.
5 Simplify and improve – and ensure that it is the plant material that is telling the story.
6 Remember that it is not so much which aspect of interpretation you choose, as there is no absolute RIGHT way, but it is how well and how clearly you portray it that matters to the judge and viewer. Here is an example of working out an interpretative exhibit:

Title: Flamenco

Colours	Plant materials	Container	Base
Red, orange, black (no green, to keep colours 'hot')	roses, carnations, oranges, blackened curved stems (to suggest wrought iron)	black, wrought iron stand	red/orange overlaid with black lace

Backing drape	Accessory	Title card	Style
Faintly suggested bull-fight poster or Moorish archway	castanets, fans, haircombs	black Gothic lettering on red	curving line arrangement or Hogarth curve to suggest rhythm of dance

(*See* ACCESSORIES, SCHEDULES, SHOWS, SHOW WORK)

JAPANESE ARRANGEMENT, *see* IKEBANA

JEWELLERY

In the late 1970s a vogue started for making jewellery from gilded or silvered dried plant materials, sometimes with the addition of pearls, beads and glitter. Brooches, rings, necklaces, ear-rings and even tiaras appeared in shows, but the jewellery was most popular as a miniature class and some exquisite work was done, both in modern and period styles.

A circle of gilded card or a small piece of hard-setting clay forms a base for the design, which should be worked out before sticking in place with a non-stringing glue, such as Pritt. Scale is of utmost importance in composing the design and tiny leaves, tendrils, calyxes and seeds with a clear-cut shape are most successful. The plant material selected should be sprayed with several coats of gold or silver before assembling. The jewellery can be worn, but is very fragile.

JUDGE

As most flower arrangement shows are competitive, qualified judges are needed and most countries with national or state flower arrangement organizations have a system of training and testing their accredited judges. Most take a practical and written examination, which can be very probing.

A judge is expected to be of the highest integrity, knowledgeable, experienced, impartial, decisive, logical, tactful and has a duty to uphold high standards of flower arrangement, to update knowledge continuously, to encourate exhibitors and to be prepared to explain decisions to the general public.

NAFAS (and some others) have a two-tier system. Judging candidates are trained and tested at area level, where it is expected that those who are successful will judge mainly within a limited radius at smaller shows, including flower club shows. After several years' experience they can apply to take their national test, and, if successful, are then likely to be invited to judge at larger shows including county and agricultural shows and national (even international) competitions. At both levels of testing NAFAS candidates judge a class orally and in writing; answer a question paper ranging over judging ethics, period styles, abstract, schedule writing, etc.; take a separate horticultural test, an interview with the adjudicators and an exercise in writing comment cards, as well as setting up an exhibit to show their own expertise.

JUDGING

Although judging criteria may vary slightly in emphasis from country to country and even from class to class in a show, the essentials that every flower arrangement judge considers are:

1 **Conformance to schedule**
Competition rules are devised to give every competitor a fair chance, so a judge must first ensure that the rules have been obeyed. Penalties for minor infringements may seem like nit-picking on the part of the judge, but consider how the other competitors in the same class may feel. If they had known that X was to be allowed leniency on one count (an arrangement an inch too high, a tiny accessory that was forbidden, plant material out of water when it should have a water supply, etc.) then the others might have acted differently and used another container, different plant material and so on. A judge must be fair to *all*.

2 **Interpretation**
This is an aspect of judging which is far less precise than deciding if the rules have been obeyed. If the title of a class calls for interpretation a judge will have done his/her homework and be aware of the many possible approaches to the theme. What is being judged is how well the plant materials, rather than just the accessories, interpret the title. It is not so much what the exhibitor has chosen to say, as how well the interpretation has been put over, that counts.

3 **Plant material**
Whilst a judge looks for flowers and leaves in good condition, clean, without blemishes, crisp and cared for, it is not horticultural excellence that counts. It is rather that everything has been well chosen with the class title in mind and that it is interesting in colour, form and texture. A profusion of expensive flowers, or fruit, is only admirable if the schedule actually calls for it.

4 **Design**
This includes colour. All the **design elements** and **design principles** (q.v.) have to be considered and whether the overall design and grouping within the space allocated is good and appropriate to the class title.

5 **Presentation**
A show entry is a presented piece of work. It is not enough to put an admirable arrangement somewhere in the space provided and leave it at that. The judge will consider the placement and use of bases, drapes, backgrounds, title cards, etc. as part of the whole. A badly finished base, dusty container, ill-written title card and creased drape will all be **downpointed** (q.v.), and thoughtful, original presentation will be rewarded.

6 **Distinction/creativity/originality**
None of these is easy to define and they generally arise from excellence in one of the other sections or a combination of several. The word 'charisma' comes to mind.

Judging systems
There are several ways of judging, and it is the organizers of the show who decide which shall be used:

Standard system: this is, in fact, ranking. First, Second and Third prizewinners are chosen, regardless of the overall standard of the class. In addition, there may be commendations: Very Highly Commended, Highly Commended and Commended. The total number of these commendations is

Judging *Judging a pedestal class in a marquee where the inelegant surroundings have to be ignored.*

usually left to the judge(s). The choice is arrived at by comparison and assessment of good and bad features in the exhibits and gradual elimination, but they are not specifically marked. This is the system most commonly used in Britain and is popular because everyone likes to know 'which is best' – even if they don't agree!

Point-scoring system: in this system judges award marks out of a pre-determined allocation of points, usually 50 or 100, e.g., Interpretation 20,

Plant material 20, Design 25, Colour 15, Presentation 10, Distinction 10 = 100. Judges deduct points, i.c., downpoint, for faults, and the skill lies in weighting these demerits. The point-scoring system is allegedly the fairest, though personally I doubt it because first, it is time-consuming, secondly, one tends to get bogged down in detail, and thirdly, it encourages negative judging – looking for faults. This is always easier, but surely less admirable, than looking for points on the credit side.

Awards system: the judge awards cards, stars or ribbons to such exhibits as are judged to have reached a good standard. There may be no awards in one class; four in another. Sometimes there are two grades of award: gold, let us say, and silver, which allows for a certain 'ranking', but still for more than one award at either level in each class. Here the difficulty is in deciding what a good standard is. Much may depend on the judge's own experience. What is 'good' for a small village show may be only mediocre by county show standards or even poor by national standards. A great deal of tact, commonsense and wide-ranging knowledge is asked of the judge. Yet arguably it produces the most satisfying results, because entries in different classes, even in one show, vary considerably. Where it may be hard to find a worthy 'First' in one class, another may contain three or four exhibits well worthy of such an award.

International judging
The formation of **WAFA**, the World Association of Flower Arrangers (q.v.), has meant that more and more exhibitors and judges are being invited to exhibit or judge in countries other than their own. It is important to remember that whilst at WAFA Shows (once every three years in the host country, at present) a simple four-rule judging formula has been agreed, individual member countries still retain their own show rules and schedule definitions for their shows 'at home'. Ultimately, even this confusion may disappear, but not for some time, I fancy.

JUNIOR FLOWER CLUBS, *see* **YOUNG FLOWER ARRANGERS**

KUBARI
A forked or crossed stick used in ikebana to support stems in a tall, narrow container.

LANDSCAPE

A landscape arrangement portrays a natural scene. 'A moment from nature is captured', is the way Jean Taylor puts it in her *Creative Flower Arrangement*. The scene may represent woodland, meadow, moor, mountain, garden, country lane, lake, riverside or seashore. This last has come to be called a 'seascape', which is hardly accurate in the sense that painters use the term, but still understandable.

Traditionally, if that is the word for a style that has developed within the last 50 years or so, a branch or driftwood is used to represent a 'tree', and flowers, leaves, ferns and such are grouped at the base as realistically as possible. The landscape is popular in spring when budding branches with tiny leaves are suitably in scale with the concept of a large tree, and small spring flowers fit well into the scene. But it is for all seasons, of course, not least at Christmas when snowy branches and robins tell another story. Wood, moss, pebbles and small **figurines** (q.v.) are acceptable additions.

If a water scene is chosen there needs to be a receptacle for the water, and then lead, rough-finish pottery or trays and dishes, painted to look as naturalistic as possible, are used.

Scale is of the utmost importance and anything too large begins to destroy the illusion. Although neither the 'tree' nor the 'lake' is lifesize, the flowers and leaves are, and a certain amount of imagination has to come into play as the viewer adds his or her own interpretation to the scene.

For the most part, these landscapes are 'arrangements', contrived in one or more containers discreetly concealed as part of the scene, and most of the plant material radiates from these containers.

In recent years, largely influenced by continental arrangers, a different kind of landscape has evolved which has more affinity, perhaps, with the plate gardens of children's classes at village shows, the Easter Gethsemane gardens in churches and *millefiore*, the flowery meads of mediaeval tapestries or Botticelli's painting, *Primavera*. Landscapes are actually created in troughs and trays which invite us to become Lilliputians and walk through them. Some have stylized hedges or serried verticals of waterside plants. They do not radiate from containers, but apparently grow up out of moss or grass turf or stones. Scale and perspective can be created by diminishing size from front to back. (*See* **PLATE (TRAY OR MOSS) GARDEN** *and colour section*)

LANGUAGE OF FLOWERS, *see* SYMBOLISM, VICTORIAN

LARGE-SCALE DESIGNS

Festivals and shows sometimes call for group and large-scale exhibits, which cause problems as everyone lacks experience in tackling them.

The team

Except for a very large affair (NAFAS stand at Chelsea Flower Show, for example), a team of three is usually best. This should comprise firstly, someone with flair, knowledge and experience; secondly, a really, dependable, competent type; and thirdly, an up-and-comer with future potential who will perhaps drive, make the coffee, keep lists, condition the plant material and learn the ropes. Either the first or second type must be the boss as it is very necessary for one person to have the final say, even though give-and-take are essential throughout.

The planning

Planning should start as early as possible; ideas discussed, research done, feelers put out for props or plant material and a detailed plan will evolve. Once this has crystallized, beware of too many last minute adjustments. Resist the temptation to embellish, but rather go for refining. At least two mock-ups, to size, are necessary, the last being fairly detailed.

The viewed-from-all-round island site

Usually staged on a platform 30 cm (12 in) or more from the ground, it may be circular or square, less often rectangular or oval. Height is often unlimited. Consider the following points:

1 The interest does not have to be equal all round, but there needs to be some feature(s) at 'the back' to focus the eye.
2 Height is essential for good balance and proportion, but it need not be central. It is often better to place the tallest point off-centre to give more depth and space for the main feature.
3 Linkage between the various parts of the exhibit is essential, even if it is depicting opposites such as 'Town and country', 'War and Peace'. Do this by taking some similar plant material through both designs, even if one is fresh and one dried; repeat some colour in both; take linking leaves, vines, ribbons, cords, etc. through the design, but beware of too much draped fabric in case it dominates. Try to link accessories by colour, or material (all wood, metal) or by association (all kitchen utensils, furnishings, nautical, etc.).
4 If there are, say, three main arrangements, don't have them all the same size or height. Let one undoubtedly predominate, put another at a different level and the third at a different height again.
5 If different arrangers are doing one arrangement each, establish the parameters for each before going too far, and see that everyone keeps within them, or balance and proportion may be lost.

The large site or alcove with backing

It often tends to be very deep for the width, or if large, then very wide for the height of the backing provided.

6 Remember that asymmetry is generally more interesting than absolute symmetry. Use the **Golden Section** (q.v.) and system of thirds to help break up the large area and site the important features. Apply the 'thirds' maxim to the height, width *and* depth.
7 Beware of a large space or hole at the centre of the overall design. It appears without warning sometimes, and rivets the attention. Adjust placings slightly to diminish it. Resist the temptation to pop something in to fill it!

Large Scale *Large-scale club exhibits in the 'Country Market' class at a NAFAS Festival.*

Overall

8 Boxes, pieces of furniture, poles and constructions are usually needed to get height and different levels. If they can be part of the design rather than something to be hidden this helps a lot. If they have to be draped or obscured then try to have plant material breaking up a large area of cover-up. It's surprising what one branch or trail can do.

9 Adopt a very selective attitude to accessories. Decide which are doing a good job and which are merely clutter. It goes without saying that for competitive show work they must not be the dominant feature. In exhibition or festival work, however, they may be the *raison d'être*, e.g., the vicar's cope, the tapestry, the carved chair.

10 Get back from the display to look at it as a whole at regular intervals. Keep the overall desired effect firmly in mind. Whilst attention to detail is important, don't get bogged down in it. (*See **colour section***)

LEAVES, *see* **FOLIAGE**

LETTERING

Whilst nothing but practice and a natural bent will produce a skilled calligrapher, arrangers sometimes need to produce pleasing lettering. Large notices such as show or class titles, classroom aids or club notices need to be:

- in letters not less than 4 cm (1½ in.) high.
- placed above people's heads, or as high as possible, to be visible.
- written in upper (capitals) and lower case (small letters), *not* in solid capitals. The irregular outline with f, g, h, y, etc. going above and below the main lines, makes it much easier to read.
- in a simple style of lettering. Gothic and some of the modern 'arty' types are not the easiest to read, especially at a distance. Clarity is all-important.
- in colours that show up well. Take a tip from road signs which have to be read at speed and use white on blue, white or yellow on dark green or black on yellow or white. Red lettering tends to 'jump', and words made up of different coloured letters are always difficult to read as some advance and some recede.

Materials and method

Coloured mounting board (from art shops and good stationers) is available in sheets 800 × 550 mm (31 × 22 in.) in a range of attractive colours. Felt pens and markers are available in waterproof or waterbased inks in a huge range of colours and a variety of tip widths by Stabilo, Staedtler, Berol, Pentel, etc. Letraset and similar dry-printing (rub-on) systems are admirable, but expensive for large scale notices.

There is no short cut to precision and perfection. Guidelines *must* be accurately ruled, but lightly; use a 2B pencil. Three guidelines are needed for each line of lettering: the base line, the line for the top of the rounded lower case letters and a top line for the top of the capitals. Spacing must be worked out and words lightly pencilled in. We all know the posters that run out of space on the right-hand side! When the lettering is quite dry use a soft eraser to rub out lines.

Programmes, schedules, hand-outs

Typewriting is adequate for the body of programmes and schedules, but not for the cover, heading or title. Letraset is ideal for this, and if one careful master copy is made it can then be photocopied.

Again, there is no short-cut to perfection and everything must be measured and spaced carefully.

If there is a club member with good handwriting, or one who has acquired an italic hand, consider asking them to write out your schedule if time and money are short. (*See* **TITLES ON EXHIBITS**)

LICHEN

Lichen is natural plant material and normally accepted as either fresh or dried, since it is difficult to tell the difference!

LINE

One of the **design elements** (q.v.) and closely allied to form. Line is attenuated form and is the feature which most often gives rhythm and direction to a design. In plant material it is most clearly seen in the curves of vines, arching sprays, tendrils and trailing plants and in the straight lines of blade-shaped leaves, stiff stems and pronounced leaf veins. These are direct lines, actually there for all to see. Indirect lines can be created in any design by repeated shapes leading the eye from each one to the next. The size may increase or diminish, but the shapes will remain similar, as seen in the familiar line of flowers in a traditional arrangement, from buds at the outline to fully open flowers at the focal point.

Vertical lines suggest action; horizontal lines, stability and repose. Diagonal or zigzag lines are exciting; gently curving lines, restful and slow moving. Thick lines are strong and masculine; thin ones weaker, more feminine. Crossed lines, whether straight or curved, suggest confusion and warring ideas.

'Line' arrangements are the opposite of massed ones. Limited plant material is used, invariably with two or three branches, stems or elongated leaves forming an outline which encloses space. More solid forms will help to focus interest, but the importance of the lines in the design will be paramount.

LITURGICAL COLOURS *see* **CHURCH FLOWERS, altar**

MADE-UP FLOWERS

The term has come to mean, in Britain at least, flowers made up from natural plant material, usually dried or preserved, *not* flowers that are entirely artificial. They are generally permitted in shows when artificial plant material is not. Check to be sure, however.

It is acceptable to glue and wire made-up flowers but you should obviously do this inconspicuously. Wire stems should be taped, or better still, slipped into a hollow stem.

The method of making up most of these flowers is shown in the diagrams for **artificial flowers** (q.v.).

Suggestions for centres: cones of various sorts ('petals' can be glued between base scales), grasses, centre bosses of rudbeckia and similar daisy flowers, glycerined clematis seedheads, beech mast, woody stamens from rhododendrons, pussy willow catkins, poppy seedheads.

Suggestions for petals: glycerined leaves such as choisya, garrya, rhododendron, eucalyptus (they can be cut and reshaped if necessary), artichoke and cardoon scales, honesty seed cases, dried *Magnolia grandiflora* petals (like suede), corncob husks.

MECHANICS

The flower arranger's term for anything that holds or supports stems in an arrangement is 'mechanics'. Those most commonly used today are pinholders, crumpled wire netting and plastic floral foams (both green for fresh arrangements and brown for preserved or artificial stems when no water supply is needed. The chart summarizes the pros and cons of each type and the diagrams (on pages I I I and I I 4) show their use in three main types of containers.

There are two golden rules to remember:

1 Whether using crumpled wire mesh or floral foam, it should come well *above* the rim of the container so that stems can be inserted at the sides as well as on top.
2 Both need wiring, tying or taping in very firmly for a large arrangement. This may not be necessary for a low table decoration, small bowl, or where the mechanics can be wedged firmly in the container.

Emergency mechanics

Occasionally one has to improvise with items readily to hand. Try criss-crossed clear adhesive tape over the top of a bowl or vase; crumpled newspaper packed into a tall vase, or shingle, sand, small stones or marbles.

The full range of mechanics likely to be needed by the average arranger is shown in the diagrams, including those for candlecups, driftwood, raised-up containers for short-stemmed flowers, topiary trees, garlands, plaques, fruit and large-scale stands.

Mechanics
Pinholders

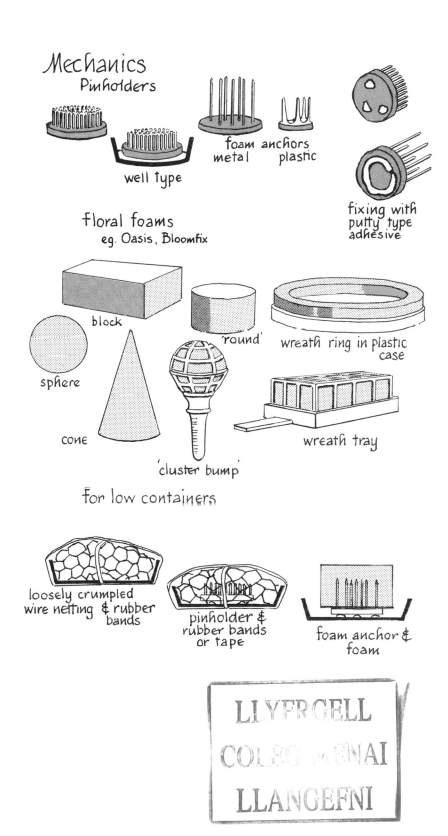

well type

foam anchors
metal   plastic

fixing with
putty type
adhesive

Floral foams
eg. Oasis, Bloomfix

block

sphere

'round'   wreath ring in plastic
case

cone

wreath tray

'cluster bump'

for low containers

loosely crumpled
wire netting & rubber
bands

pinholder &
rubber bands
or tape

foam anchor &
foam

Type of support	Where to buy	What to look for	How to fix it
Pinholder (also called a 'kenzan', needlepoint holder)	club sales tables, florists, garden centres	Heavy lead base (suction type not reliable) Close-set, sharp, rustless, metal pins, not less than 2 cm ($\frac{3}{4}$ in.) long Pins covering all area of base. Buy 7.5 cm (3 in.) for general use and 7 cm ($2\frac{3}{4}$in.) for candlecups	To a *dry* container with good quality Plasticine or Oasis-fix strip
Well-pinholder	as above	As above and *deep* enough for water to cover pins	Not necessary
Wire-netting (also called wire mesh, chicken wire)	hardware shops and garden centres, ironmongers	5 cm (2 in.) mesh for crumpling Fine gauge wire is easier to bend and use Plastic-covered type is not necessary and tends to show more $\frac{1}{2} \times 1$ metre ($\frac{1}{2} \times 1$ yd) sufficient for three sizeable containers 2.5 cm (1 in.) mesh for a cap over foam	Cut off selvedge Crumple to provide several layers of holes Tie into containers like a parcel with string, or florist's reel wire, or use two rubber bands crossed over the container or Oasis tape. Attach 2.5 cm (1 in.) mesh, used as a cap, with reel wire
Water-retaining foams e.g. Oasis	club sales tables, florists, garden centres	Most types are efficient If needed for fresh plant material be sure to buy the water-absorbing type (green) and not the one for dry use only (brown). A large block for cutting into smaller pieces is most economical. Cut with a knife, wet or dry	Soak in deep water until the foam is level with the surface of the water. After soaking 1. Place on an 'anchor' (see below) fixed to the container like a pinholder 2. Wedge firmly into neck of narrower containers or into inexpensive plastic or ceramic dishes sold for the purpose 3. Secure if desired with a cap of wire netting placed over it and fixed to the container
Foam anchors (Metal)	As above	Heavy base Long prongs to give good support	As for pinholders
Plastic known as 'prongs' or 'frogs'	As above	Usually 4-pronged about 2.5 cm (1 in.) diameter	As for pinholders

Advantages	Disadvantages
Lasts a lifetime Provides weight for stability Holds heavy branches, thick stems and heavy flower and seedheads Available in many shapes and sizes	Expensive outlay but essential item. Unsuitable for very thin stems (e.g. freesias) Used alone it only holds a limited quantity of stems Difficult to get a down-flowing line with stiff plant material
No additional container needed Takes up minimum space Easily hidden by plant material Inexpensive and lasts a long time Not eye-catching and easily concealed by plant material A cap of netting gives extra support	Expensive outlay and often an ordinary pinholder fixed in a shallow tin serves as well Not always easy to buy in small quantities May scratch or rust-mark precious containers Does not give complete security for heavy stems unless used with a pinholder Hard on the hands!
Allows stems to be placed at any angle even with cut ends pointing upwards when a down-flowing line is needed Allows a very shallow container to be used Ideal for fine stems, e.g., freesias, carnations Never smells of stagnant water Can be bought in large bricks or rounds Avoids having loose water to spill during transport, on dining tables, for gifts Wrapped in thin polythene, it can be used for hanging arrangements such as plaques and mobiles	More expensive as it can only be used 2 or 3 times before it breaks up. Top surface dries out quickly Clogs some soft stems like anemones, daffodils, narcissi Can be difficult to hide if large pieces are used Not adequate alone for large, tall or heavy arrangements – needs pinholder and/or wire-netting as well If allowed to dry out completely will not take up much water again therefore store in a plastic bag to keep damp Can soon be honeycombed by inexpert arranger and so breaks up Stems should be pushed in only far enough to be held firmly
Adds weight for stability Long lasting	More expensive than plastic
Cheap, therefore disposable Useful for gift arrangments and in hospitals Good for small containers	No weight to help stability Prongs snap easily if forced Inadequate support for arrangements over 25 cm (10 in.) high

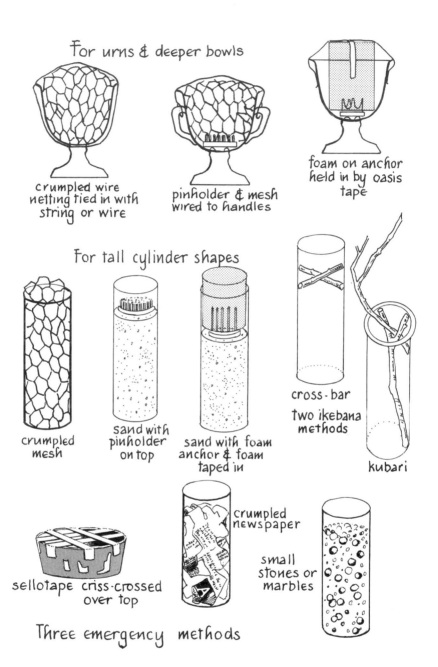

For urns & deeper bowls

crumpled wire
netting tied in with
string or wire

pinholder & mesh
wired to handles

foam on anchor
held in by oasis
tape

For tall cylinder shapes

crumpled
mesh

sand with
pinholder
on top

sand with foam
anchor & foam
taped in

cross-bar

two ikebana
methods

kubari

sellotape criss-crossed
over top

crumpled
newspaper

small
stones or
marbles

Three emergency methods

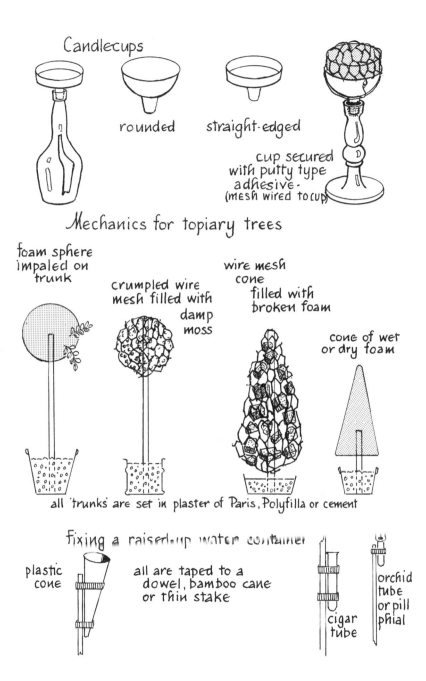

Candlecups

rounded

straight-edged

cup secured
with putty type
adhesive·
(mesh wired to cup)

Mechanics for topiary trees

foam sphere
impaled on
trunk

crumpled wire
mesh filled with
damp
moss

wire mesh
cone
filled with
broken foam

cone of wet
or dry foam

all 'trunks' are set in plaster of Paris, Polyfilla or cement

Fixing a raised-up water container

plastic
cone

all are taped to a
dowel, bamboo cane
or thin stake

cigar
tube

orchid
tube
or pill
phial

Supports for branches & driftwood

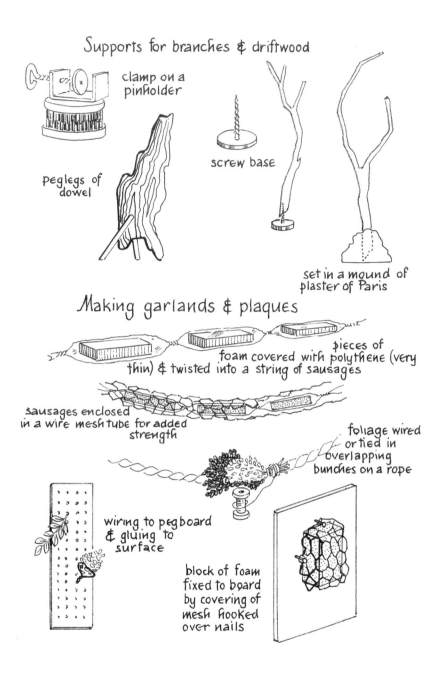

clamp on a
pinholder

peglegs of
dowel

screw base

set in a mound of
plaster of Paris

Making garlands & plaques

pieces of
foam covered with polythene (very thin) & twisted into a string of sausages

sausages enclosed
in a wire mesh tube for added
strength

foliage wired
or tied in
overlapping
bunches on a rope

wiring to pegboard
& gluing to
surface

block of foam
fixed to board
by covering of
mesh hooked
over nails

Fixing fruit

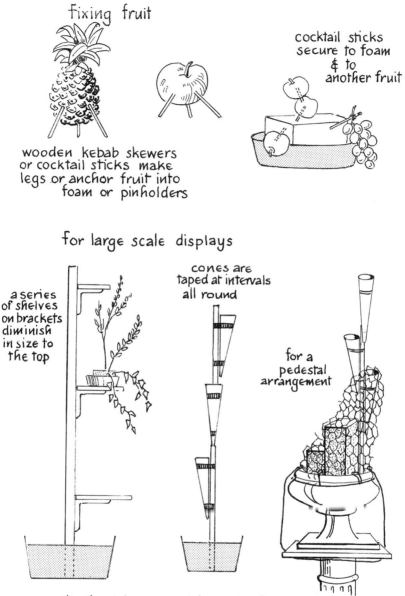

cocktail sticks
secure to foam
& to
another fruit

wooden kebab skewers
or cocktail sticks make
legs or anchor fruit into
foam or pinholders

for large scale displays

a series
of shelves
on brackets
diminish
in size to
the top

cones are
taped at intervals
all round

for a
pedestal
arrangement

sturdy stakes are set in cement

MECHANICS, COVERING

There are usually enough flowers and leaves to obscure mechanics used for massed arrangements. It is not necessary to hide every square millimetre, but areas of foam, netting or pinholder noticeable from a reasonable viewing distance are unsightly, and a competition judge will down-point for them. In sparse modern and abstract styles obscuring the mechanics is more difficult because even one extra leaf can ruin the design. Consider using moss, stones, pebbles, chippings, broken windscreen glass, shells, bark, driftwood, coffee beans, or small pieces of washed coal. Deep, inverted box bases with holes cut to allow the plant material to come through from a pinholder below can be effective for abstracts. Foam can be painted to match containers, or wrapped in fresh, dried or glycerined leaves secured with wire 'hairpins'; for Christmas and party arrangements crêpe paper or kitchen foil may be suitable. Small tubes to hold water for one or two flowers can be taped behind wood or spathes or pushed into hollow stems, hollows in driftwood or inside seedheads.

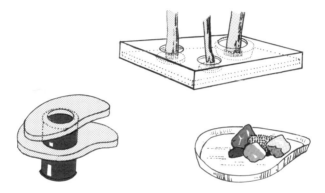

Mechanics, covering *Three ways of hiding mechanics:* (top) *inverted box base with holes for stems;* (left) *tiered bases on tins with a pinholder in the top one;* (right) *stones used to hide a pinholder in a low dish.*

MINIATURE

This is a small-scale arrangement or exhibit which, in competitive work, has a maximum stated measurement. It is usually expressed as 'not more than X cm/in. overall' or 'not more than X cm/in. in width, depth and height'. The diagonal length does not count.

Under NAFAS rules the measurement is 10 cm (4 in.); in other countries it may be slightly more or less. It is vital at a show not to exceed the limit, yet more miniatures are disqualified for being oversize than any other type of entry. Work well within the limit stated, e.g., within 9 cm ($3\frac{1}{2}$ in.) if the limit stated is 10 cm (4 in.). Stems move and some can even grow, so allow a margin for error. Miniatures are preferably staged at eye-level, but this is not always possible.

The arranger who works in miniature has a number of problems, but expense, at least, is not one of them!

Scale

This is of utmost importance and everything used must be in scale with every other component. Faults in scale show up so clearly in a tiny doll's

Miniature and Petite *Miniature and petite arrangements; a 50 pence piece indicates the scale.*

house type arrangement and the commonest are: (1) having too big a container, (2) having the largest central flowers or leaves just *too* large, and (3) using an unnecessarily large base or one that is too thick. It is often said that a photograph will most quickly show if the scale is right. In a photograph, without something well-known (coin, stamp, thimble) placed nearby for comparison, it should be impossible to detect whether the arrangement is 3 inches or 3 feet high if everything is in scale.

Water
Because containers and mechanics are so tiny, an adequate water supply for fresh plant material is not easy. Tiny pieces of floral foam dry out quickly. For show work select long-lasting plant materials and, to avoid fragile stems being broken so that they cannot take up water, use a needle or pin to make holes in the floral foam first. Misting with a very fine spray helps to keep everything moist.

Handling
Use sharp nail scissors for cutting and tweezers if you can, to avoid too much clumsy handling.

Sources
For containers: small bottle tops, buttons, shells, coins, doll's house furniture and china.
For plant material: florets and leaflets which have their own little stems,

rockery and alpine plants, ferns, cupressus, rue, thyme, marjoram, heather, alchemilla, crocosmia, saxifrage, berberis and golden rod.

Miniatures may, of course, be in any style: landscape, massed traditional, period, free-style, abstract, a plaque or a picture, unless a show schedule specifically requests a particular type. (*See* **PETITE**)

MOBILE, STABILE AND STAMOBILE

These three types of structures are considered together because they all evolved from the work of Alexander Calder, an American sculptor and abstract painter. His work in this field in the 1930s was a combination of sculpture and engineering. A *stabile* is a rigid structure/sculpture which gives the illusion that at any moment it might take off and move; a *mobile* is suspended and its individual parts move independently in air currents. A *stamobile*, as the name implies, is a combination of the two, a standing structure with one or more movable parts suspended or springing from it.

In flower arrangement such structures are normally classed as 'abstracts', though many do have a distinctly naturalistic look about the individual parts. A stamobile, for example, is sometimes seen at shows as a chunky piece of driftwood, providing the standing part, with seedheads, flowers or leaves suspended from it on threads of cotton or nylon, to twist and turn as the air moves. Not easy to construct, they have had a limited appeal, and indeed two classes for a stamobile at the NAFAS Festival 1987 were cancelled because of lack of competitors. The designs below are by Alexander Calder.

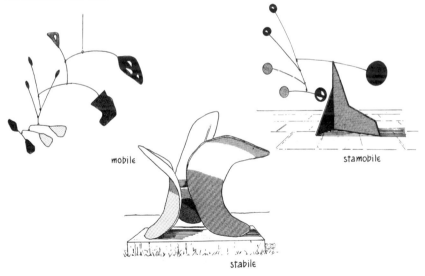

mobile

stamobile

stabile

MODERN ARRANGEMENTS, *see* FREE-STYLE

MOSS

Before floral foams were invented, moss was the most important water-retaining material used by arrangers and florists. It is still used today for 'mossing' wreath frames, for flower balls and for garlands. Dried moss, re-soaked and firmly packed, will hold stems well and provide enough moisture to keep flowers fresh.

NAFAS

NAFAS, the National Association of Flower Arrangement Societies of Great Britain, formed in 1959, now has over 100,000 members in more than 1,400 flower clubs in Britain and in affiliated groups overseas. Members are mostly women, though there is an increasing number of men. Most members are amateur arrangers, not professional florists.

The Association was recognized as a charity (No. 289038) in 1984 'to advance public education in the art of flower arrangement and related subjects and to further any other charitable purpose.' Over the years NAFAS and its clubs have raised several million pounds for charity by organizing flower shows and other events, and festivals in churches and stately homes. (*See* **APPENDIX: ADDRESSES** *and* **MAGAZINES**)

NAFAS TEACHERS' ASSOCIATION

Formed in 1969 by the NAFAS Education Committee to help and unite flower arrangers who teach the art and craft of flower arrangement, whether at their clubs, in their own homes or employed by local education authorities. No qualification, other than membership of a NAFAS club, is required. Members receive a magazine, *Insight*, three times a year and other small publications from time to time, have the chance to attend residential courses and may borrow teaching slides. Write to NAFAS for details. (*See* **APPENDIX: ADDRESSES**)

NCCPG

The National Council for the Conservation of Plants and Gardens was formed in the early 1980s in Britain under the auspices of The Royal Horticultural Society, to try to conserve garden plants of value and interest fast disappearing from gardens and nursery catalogues.

One of the Council's priorities was to establish national collections of plants in different parts of the country. There are now over 300, in botanic and private gardens, commercial nurseries and agricultural colleges.

Local county and regional support groups help by surveying local gardens, collating nursery garden catalogues and plant lists and organizing fund-raising events.

NICHE

A foldable, triptych-like alcove of painted plywood, hardboard or stiff cardboard. They are popular for show staging as they are easy to set up and store in a comparatively small space. A convenient size for club shows has a back panel 90 cm (3 ft) high by 75 cm (2 ft 6 in.) or 60 cm (2 ft) wide with folding wings about 25 cm (10 in.) wide which can be splayed out if needed. Suitable colours are blue-grey and grey-green.

In large shows in recent years niches have become less popular as more open staging is preferred in the centre of a hall, but they are still very practical if used against the walls. They help both competitors, judges and visitors to concentrate on one exhibit at a time.

NINETEEN TWENTIES AND THIRTIES

The period between the First and Second World Wars saw a great change in life styles, with the emancipation of women and their shorter dresses and hair styles; gramophones and the jazz age; the cinema and the influence of Hollywood films; Art Deco styles; the rise of the suburban house and garden; and the interest in home decoration.

Settings
White and beige walls with dark oak or grained and varnished woodwork; floral or 'folk-weave' furnishings; opaque glass light fittings; and tiled fireplaces without the former wooden surrounds were all popular. The Art Deco style influenced many domestic articles in the thirties: tables, rugs, cups and saucers, mirrors, fabric design, ornaments, the new cocktail-shakers, cigarette cases, lipstick cases and powder compacts.

Colours
With beige or oatmeal as background colours, orange became exceedingly popular, as did purple, bright green, blue and yellow. In fashionable circles glossy black and silver with cream or white were considered *soigné* and chic.

Plant material
As orange was so popular, it was natural that marigolds (calendula and tagetes), nasturtiums and tawny and rust-coloured chrysanthemums should be among the favourite flowers, with Chinese lanterns (*Physalis sylvestris*) and orange-berried iris pods (*I. foetidissima*). Michaelmas daisies provided a link with purple colourings. Wild flowers, through the seasons,

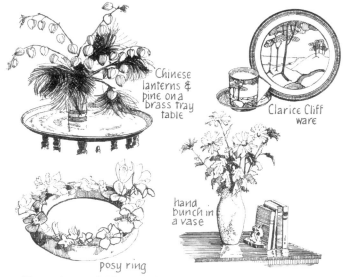

Nineteen Twenties and Thirties *Arrangements and furnishings characteristic of the 1920s and '30s.*

were brought indoors to be arranged, also 'sticky buds' of the horse chestnut, pussy willow, beech leaves and pressed bracken. Most of the other flowers we know and grow today were available, though perhaps generally smaller. Carnations, asparagus fern and gypsophila came from the florist.

Containers
Shallow bowls, coloured black inside; cut glass bowls with netted metal covers; frosted glass in geometric styles; hand-thrown pottery; earthenware jugs with a glazed rim; brass, copper and pewter; posy rings in pottery; Clarice Cliff and Susie Cooper ware; pottery troughs in beige or eau-de-nil.

Arrangements and uses
1 Roses, dahlias, etc. floating in shallow bowls, often round a figurine.
2 One type of flower simply arranged: daffodils, tulips, marigolds, sweet peas.
3 Jugs/vases of blossom cut to force indoors.
4 Simple landscape designs and plate gardens with Chinese ornaments.
5 Constance Spry, in the 1930s, was becoming well-known for her 'mixed' groups, all-foliage arrangements and adventurous use of lichened branches, lilies, artichokes and anthuriums in urns and tazzas.
6 Table decorations, under the influence of Mrs Beeton, were lighter and less formal with place mats used instead of cloths. Much more emphasis was placed on matching and toning colour schemes.
7 Pottery wall vases enjoyed a vogue as they did not require many flowers and were probably arranged without any mechanics.

Accessories
Candles became far more colourful and were used as decorative items on dinner tables. Figurines were becoming directly associated with flower arrangements rather than just standing nearby as ornaments. The crocheted or linen mat under a vase was still much in evidence.

Mechanics
The glass 'rose' was still widely used and the netted covers of rose bowls. Constance Spry used crumpled wire netting. Otherwise moss, sand, stones or gravel were fairly effective supports (See MECHANICS).

Symbolism
Only remnants of the 'Language of Flowers' remained, but the red poppy became symbolic of the dead of the First World War. (See PERIOD ARRANGING, ART DECO)

NOT ACCORDING TO SCHEDULE
The dreaded letters 'N.A.S.' (not according to schedule) on a card by his/her exhibit is every competitor's nightmare. Yet it happens to the best and most experienced of exhibitors. Some factor, large or small, has been overlooked, and in fairness to the other exhibitors in that class a judge has to disqualify (see JUDGING), under NAFAS rules at least. There are many judges who would prefer down-pointing, but the difficulty is in determining by how much. A very good exhibit could still emerge as a prize-winner in spite of very severe down-pointing. It is usually regarded as unfair if any exhibitor who breaks the rules is allowed to win.

OASIS

Oasis is the trademark of various floral products from the firm of Smithers-Oasis, but the word is best known to arrangers as the green **floral foam** (q.v.) which holds water and the brown foam for dried and artificial stems. All foams tend to be called 'oasis', whatever their origin.

Oasis fix is a green putty-like strip sold in reels (*see* **TOOLS & EQUIPMENT**) with a strong adhesive quality for fixing pinholders, candle-cups, etc. It is not easy to remove after use, and it is best to scrape as much as possible away, with a blunt knife and, then remove the remainder with a rag soaked in white spirit (turpentine substitute), dry cleaner spirit such as Beaucaire, or oily nail-lacquer remover. Beware of using Oasis fix with fabric; it is then almost impossible to remove.

Oasis tape is a tough, dark khaki-green tape available in 0.5 or 1 cm ($\frac{3}{16}$ or $\frac{3}{8}$ in.) widths for securing foam or wire mesh in containers, and various other uses. Remove any residual stickiness as for Oasis fix above. (*See* **TAPE**)

OIL

Wiping evergreen leaves with a pad of rag or cotton wool dipped in oil (cooking, machine or general purpose) removes dirt (you'd be surprised how much) and gives a lustrous sheen. Wipe off any surplus. Leaves should never look oily.

ORIGINALITY

In Britain we tend to say 'originality' whereas **creativity** (q.v.) is more favoured in America. The words are virtually interchangeable.

Since there is very little that is entirely new or original under the sun, originality in flower arrangement is likely to be in the use of well-known materials in a new way, or an unusual combination, a fresh approach to presentation, an unexpected balance, a different viewpoint, and so on.

It is not enough just to do something different at a show; that something different must be done well – adventurously conceived, finely executed and immaculately presented – to earn marks for originality. Remember that what is trite and hackneyed now was once original, so don't complain if someone takes and adapts one of your 'original' ideas. It is said that anything with just 3 per cent of one's own expression can be called original!

OVERALL

Until recently a term applied in show schedules to the maximum permitted measurements of miniature and petite arrangements, e.g., 'not more than X cm/in. overall'. It is now considered more accurate to say 'not exceeding X cm/in. in width, depth and height'. In either wording, the length of the *diagonal* measurement is to be ignored.

PACKING

Packing plant materials, containers, etc. to take to a show, festival or demonstration requires care. See that all plant material is well **conditioned** (q.v.) first.

Flowers: If travelling by car decide what sort of carrier to use:
(a) *Tall side-handled buckets* are best as they give most protection, but they need to stand in a carrier of some sort – a home-made wooden frame or a flower-box lid with holes cut to take the buckets. If no carrier is possible, see that the buckets are wedged firmly, otherwise they will fall over when you corner or brake sharply. Only half-fill them with water.
(b) *Flower boxes* pack well in a car. Line them first with thin (dry-cleaner's) **polythene** (q.v.) and pack the flowers top to tail, fairly firmly, so that they are not crushed, but provide support for each other. Cover with polythene and mist-spray over the polythene to increase humidity, before putting on the lid.

Foliage: Conditioned foliage travels well in polythene bags secured with a wire twist. Avoid leaving them in full sun or the bags become a closed greenhouse! Taller branches/sprays can travel in buckets or boxes.

Containers and accessories: Wrap in sheets of bubble-plastic for extra padding, then in a box, carry-bag or basket.

Fabrics: Roll fabrics on a cardboard tube, no matter how good-tempered they seem. Wrap the tube in polythene or, better still, make a long bag for it. *N.B. put your name on everything*

If you have to park for long *en route*, go to some lengths to find shade in summer. When you stop for refreshment, check the flowers and leaves as well.

Freighting by plane: Here the handling of boxes is out of your own hands. The Natal judges are experts at air-freight packing and they pull foliage stems through the cut-off legs of tights (nylons) or stockings to keep leaf sprays in shape. Pack as for the car otherwise and tie up the box securely and attach necessary labels. Make sure that you know (from the Embassy) what plant materials will be allowed into the country. Some have very strict rules indeed, New Zealand and America for example. Carry any precious containers with you as cabin baggage.

PAINTS

Arrangers use a surprising number of paints for different jobs so it is as well to know the full range.

Acrylic: also called polymer. A water-based plastic paint which dries to a waterproof finish. Faster drying than oil paints. Use on paper, card, masonry, canvas, clay, acetate fabrics, etc. – any non-oily surface in fact. Apply with a brush. Clean brushes and remove drips with water before paint sets.

Blackboard: a hard, oil-based, waterproof paint with a roughish, matt finish. In black or dark green. Apply with a brush. Solvent: white spirit.

▲ *Car spray:* metallic and gloss finishes in a vast range of colours. Very quick drying; covering capacity not good, but invaluable for colouring dried plant materials and if used lightly soaks in to give a matt finish. Can be used in combinations of colours for subtle effects. Often sold off cheaply at car accessory shops as car colour ranges change. Solvent: white spirit.

Emulsion: the matt, egg-shell and silk finish paint used for household decorating. Easy to use with brush or roller; washes out with water before paint sets. Huge range of colours (e.g., Dulux 'Colorizer'). The small trial pots are useful for small areas. Good for niches, backgrounds or containers but plastic or shiny surfaces must be roughened with medium sand-paper first.

Enamel: small tins of 'Humbrol' from a wide range at model shops are good for detail finishes or smallish areas of strong, bold colour. Very hard finish. Solvent: white spirit.

▲ *Floral and decorative sprays:* like Oasis and European Aerosols can be used on fresh and dried plant materials. Lightly used on dried materials they are attractive, but sprayed solidly the effect is artificial.

Goldfinger: a rub-on paste, sold in tubes, which can be applied with a finger or pad of cotton wool, then buffed to a shine. Several different shades of gold, and other metals, are obtainable. Good for highlights and small decorative features on containers, accessories and sturdy seedheads. Can be thinned with white spirit and applied with a brush.

* *Gouache:* an opaque, water-based paint which spreads easily and covers well. Poster paint is the cheaper version. Not water-proof when dry.

Hair sprays/lacquer: useful for spraying on bullrushes, artichoke heads, pampas grass, wild clematis seedheads and any which tend to 'fluff' when mature. Solvent: methylated spirit.

Matt (or gloss) sprays: e.g., U-Spray. Available from hardware shops in a limited range of colours including black and white. Better covering capacity than car sprays. Solvent: white spirit.

▲ *Metallic:* sprays in gold, silver and copper are available everywhere at Christmas time and now during most of the year at hardware shops, etc. Woolworth's is one of the best. Tins are more economical, but less quick drying. Metallic paint can be bought as a size to mix with loose powder, or ready mixed, at art shops. Solvent: white spirit.

Nail lacquer: useful in bright colours to name or initial pinholders, scissors, buckets, containers. Solvent: acetone or polish remover from chemists.

Oils: (*a*) artist's oil paint is sold in tubes at art shops – only for use on an impervious surface; (*b*) household, gloss or matt is available in an extensive range at hardware shops. Both are slow drying. Solvent: white spirit.

Polymer: see Acrylic

Polyurethane varnish: available in matt or gloss finish. Seals porous surfaces, including wood and pottery containers. Solvent: white spirit.

* *Poster: see Gouache.* Not waterproof when dry.

* *Watercolour:* water-based as the name implies. Sold in tubes or small tablets at art shops. Suitable for small areas and touching up dried and pressed plant materials. No use on a smooth, impervious surface. Not waterproof when dry.

Wood stain: Ronseal makes a range of wood stains from pale pine to antique oak. Useful for altering the colour of driftwood and wooden bases.

* Gouache, poster and watercolours can be sprayed with water-colour varnish to give a waterproof finish.
▲ These paint sprays should be kept away from direct heat. They are best used at room temperature and must be shaken very thoroughly before, and again during, use. To prevent the nozzle clogging after use, turn the tin upside down and continue spraying till no more comes out. If a nozzle does become clogged, it can be twisted off the can and left to soak in white spirit (a solvent) to remove dried paint.

PAPER SCULPTURE

A form of modelling in paper, of use to flower arrangers in making accessories, backgrounds and 'title cards' for shows. A very sharp craft knife, scissors and a metal ruler are essential. The basic techniques are:

1 Cutting paper with a knife and with scissors.
2 Scoring, by drawing a sharp knife across the paper to cut just the surface, so that it can be folded along a crisp line.
3 Bending to give a rounded shape to the paper, by holding it down with the edge of a ruler and pulling the paper up from under, at about 45°.
4 Curling is done in much the same way, but with narrow pieces of paper. Here the blade of a knife or opened scissors is pulled sharply along the length of the paper held firmly in the other hand.
  Flowers, leaves, birds, faces, scrolls, etc., can be made in relief or 3-D.
Consult a good paper sculpture textbook for patterns.

PEDESTAL ARRANGEMENT

With the superbly varied foliage and flowers available in British gardens and the predilection of NAFAS arrangers for massed designs with flowing lines, it was natural that the pedestal arrangement should become their hallmark. It provides a splendid show piece for church, stately home, hall, exhibition and, on a more modest scale, the lounge at home. Pedestals are also movable, so can be set up exactly where needed. The pedestal itself is usually a column or plinth of wood, marble, etc., or a stand in wrought metal about 1 metre (3–4 ft) high. The container may be an urn or vase, but is often a low bowl or tin concealed by the arrangement, which will be about 2 metres (6–7 ft) high when finished. These measurements are for the average church pedestal.

The security and adequacy of the mechanics are obviously of great importance and a typical set-up is shown under **MECHANICS** on page 117.

Most pedestal arrangements are triangular in shape, symmetrical and massed, though any shape or style is possible. The typical 'English' pedestal relies on an outline of foliage, blossom or spikes of flowers, with branches or trailing foliages like ivy, flowing down from the container as much as halfway down the pedestal. Larger leaves and bushier foliages fill in centrally and help conceal the mechanics. The flowers more or less follow the outlines; buds and small flowers on the longest stems are positioned towards the outside and the largest flowers in the centre to make a focal area. Because this is a larger-scale arrangement it does not necessarily need more plant material, but flowers and leaves that are larger and on longer stems. When only short-stemmed flowers are available (e.g., in spring) a cone or cigar tube taped to a garden cane can be used to lengthen a flower stem and take the flower colour right up into the design.

Pedestal *A traditionally elegant pedestal arranged by members of the Surrey Area of NAFAS.*

PERENNIAL

A plant which survives for several (often many) years with new herbaceous growth each year. Perennials provide many of the arrangers' great stand-bys, such as hostas, delphiniums, alchemilla, ferns, heathers and the like. Increase them by root division and beg pieces from friends.

Accessory A well-used accessory. The scale and colour link with the plant material, and the branch of contorted hazel creates a suitably oriental setting. Every item plays its part, including the cleverly-staged bases. (*Arranger: Dorothy Bye, Aldershot.*)

Christmas A fireplace decorated with festive evergreens, cones and artificial poinsettias.

Colour Flowers and candles in a brass candelabra with a dish of fruit. The analogous colours based on orange have their complementary colour, blue, as a background.

Drying and preserving A rich variety of dried and preserved materials, both as an arrangement and as a plaque, interprets the work of the wood carver Grinling Gibbons. (*Arranger: Peggy Thorpe, Dore, Sheffield.*)

Foliage A basket of foliage showing a range of colour, shape and texture.

Fruit Fruit, vegetables and cones displayed on a large basketry base.

Home, Flowers in the Flowers from a late summer garden, arranged on a tallboy, pick up some of the colourings from the plate standing nearby. (*Arranger: Yvonne Toynbee, Wadhurst, Kent.*)

right **Free-style** A free-style/abstract design, *Seascape with yellow fish*, took its inspiration from a Paul Klee painting. It shows the use of only two types of plant material; a multi-opening container and the backing are used to support part of the design.

Home, Flowers in the Glycerined, dried (some colour-sprayed) and artificial flowers and leaves for a winter arrangement.

Landscape *At the edge of the wood*, a landscape influenced by both the plate garden and the continental style.

right **Large scale** A large-scale club exhibit at a spring show interpreting *Country Market* with a minimum of accessories. The basket containers set the scene with a well-chosen gingham drape. The pheasant feathers, echoing the shape of the dock (rumex) seedheads, fruit, vegetables and flowers tell the rest of the story. (*Arranged by Preston (Brighton) Flower Club.*)

Victorian A table dressed in Victorian style with midsummer flowers, ferns and fruit.

PERIOD ARRANGING

The interest in period-style arranging has developed in line with the universal interest in conservation, antiques and the preservation of our heritage.

The value of studying and attempting to arrange in period style is that:

1 It broadens the whole subject of flower arranging, leading to an interest in decor, architecture, paintings, gardens, literature, carvings and embroideries. In any of these, clues to the contemporary use of flowers may be found.

2 It helps our understanding of today's modern and abstract styles because we see how they have evolved from the social climate and artistic developments of the times, just as historical styles have done.

3 It may be useful for inspiration when decorating a stately home, creating an exhibition piece or décor for a play or special occasion.

4 There is always something of the excitement of the chase in coming across lasting clues, visual or written, to an art that is so ephemeral. We are fascinated to learn that pollen grains can tell us that 46,000 years ago Neanderthal man decorated his graves with flowers, or that when King Tutankhamun's tomb was opened in the 1920s, the flower collar that he wore had been perfectly dried and preserved for some 3,000 years!

Atmosphere or authenticity?
Authentic re-creations of period flower arrangements are seldom possible, mainly because plants have changed through hybridizing. Period containers may be valuable, unobtainable antiques; pictures and descriptions may be slight, even non-existent. For the most part one is interpreting the style of the chosen period with as much regard as possible for the colours and materials available at that time. Show schedules should try to avoid titles that appear to call for authenticity, e.g., a Victorian posy, a Roman garland, but ask rather for an exhibit 'in the style of', or 'inspired by'.

Information is available, to a greater or lesser degree, about flower arranging (meaning the use of flowers and foliage in its very widest sense) in the following periods which each have a separate entry:

BC 3000–332	Egyptian
600–146	Greek
AD 28–325	Roman
395–1453	Byzantine
960–1912	Chinese
1400–1600	Renaissance
1485–1600	Tudor
1600–1800	Dutch/Flemish
1620–1800	American Colonial
1714–1830	Georgian
1715–1774	French Rococo
1830–1900	Victorian
1900–1914	Edwardian
1920–1939	Nineteen twenties and thirties

(*See also* **ART DECO, ART NOUVEAU** and **TWENTIETH CENTURY**)

Containers

There are good plastic replicas of period urns, cherub containers, tazzas, etc., and junk shops, street markets and car-boot sales are happy hunting grounds for bits and pieces. Spray paints, stick-on motifs, impact adhesives and a little ingenuity make it possible to contrive very authentic-looking containers. Black shoe polish brushed on, then almost completely buffed away, is useful for the ageing process.

Mechanics

Whilst most present day arrangers will use floral foam for the mechanics, it may allow a flowing line not possible in the actual period and sometimes it is well to use the mechanics of the age, if they are known, e.g., sand or moss or the old glass 'rose' with holes to take the stems.

Colour

Colours are important in giving period atmosphere, especially the combinations in which they are used. No previous era has delighted in the subtle, toning colours of the present-day British mass designs. The Byzantine rich jewel colours and the glowing polychromatic hues of the Dutch flowerpieces are less easy to combine in a harmonious whole. Note how much greenery was used; the quantity can affect the other colours by toning them down too much.

Accessories

Exact dating is not required, but the overall style and shape need to be more or less accurate to give the right atmosphere. Title cards lettered, and even worded, in period style, help to create this, as does the use of the right kind of wood or fabric.

Plant material

Generally flowers and leaves were smaller and less colourful than they are today, so select smaller varieties if there is a choice. For classroom work and in the home substitutes should be accepted – single spray chrysanthemums for daisies; hydrangeas for viburnum 'snowballs'; thalictrum foliage for maidenhair fern; and many more. Except in show work, artificial flowers may be acceptable for crown imperials, tulips, and iris which all have a very distinctive shape and are such a significant feature of Dutch/Flemish paintings but not available throughout the year, or not available at all in some countries.

Finally, the period pieces are being presented for twentieth-century eyes accustomed to twentieth-century ideas. There will always have to be a compromise between the two. As with any other form of interpretative arranging (for that is what this is) it is the way that the plant material is used which is of the greatest importance. Period accessories, however authentic, do not make a present day triangular design into a period piece.

PETITE

A small arrangement, but not as small as a miniature. Under NAFAS rules it means an exhibit not exceeding 23 cm (9 in.) in width, depth and height. In the home, petites are just the size for a desk, bedside or dressing table and they are about right for hospital gifts. Less fiddly to arrange, they do not present as many problems as miniatures, but *scale* is still the most important thing to bear in mind. The range of suitably-sized plant material is obviously much wider, but the commonest faults with petites are the same as those given for miniatures. (*See* picture, page 119)

PHOTOGRAPHY

Modern colour photography has provided flower arrangers with a means of recording their ephemeral art. One must always remember that it reduces three-dimensional forms to two dimensions because there is no real depth.

Before buying film or ordering photographs to be taken, decide what their purpose is and choose accordingly. If you want snap shots or pictures for your own record, use normal print film. If you want better quality shots (for reproduction in a book or magazine perhaps) then use slide film for transparencies; large format 6 × 6 cm ($2\frac{1}{4}$ × $2\frac{1}{4}$ in.) is better than 35 mm film.

Choosing film according to light conditions
If you are shooting with a flash or in bright daylight use daylight film or artificial light film with an 85B filter. If you are shooting in artificial light use artificial light film (tungsten film) or daylight film plus an 80B filter.

Problems and remedies
For good results attention to detail is absolutely essential, especially for photographs intended for reproduction.

Height: the camera should usually be level with the centre of interest of the arrangement

Shadows: eliminate confusing shadows whenever possible, by avoiding direct sun rays or bouncing the flash off a white ceiling or wall, or using reflecting umbrellas or more than one light source. Alternatively increase the gap between the arrangement and the background and angle the lighting.

Candles: make sure they are vertical with wicks tweaked up, or even better, alight.

Curtains: they must hang straight and in soft folds to avoid a striped look.

Backgrounds: no creases, marks or raw edges. Use matt, not shiny materials – display felts, uncrushable fabrics, and studio background papers are suitable.

Decor: if using a room setting choose a plain background. Remove any clutter; avoid radiators and light switches; move furnishings to compose best picture.

Plant material: if arranging specially for photography, use less than usual to enable the forms to be seen. Little recession is necessary and 'backs' do not need filling in. Make sure there are no flowers or leaves drooping onto the base.

Containers: should stand square to the edge of the picture, especially important for those with feet or handles.

Highlights: avoid distracting shine or reflections on containers and accessories.

Lighting: strip lighting distorts colours unless special filters are used.

Faults: check from the camera viewpoint for visible mechanics, drooping plant material, poorly finished bases, creases, crooked candles, design faults, pieces of fluff, dropped leaves, spots, water marks, cracks, etc.

At shows: remove all cards, rosettes, etc., *but replace them carefully afterwards.* Avoid radiators, 'No Smoking' signs, etc. It may be necessary to raise the camera height to make sure that the top of the arrangement is within the niche in the finished picture.

PINHOLDER

The pinholder, needlepoint holder or kenzan, to give it its Japanese name, came to us with ikebana from Japan, but it was not commonly available in Britain until the 1950s. The most commonly used shape is circular, but pinholders may also be square, rectangular or crescent-shaped and in sizes from tiny 1 cm ($\frac{1}{2}$ in.) to 15 cm (6 in.) in diameter.

While ikebana arrangers do not fix the kenzan to the container, most western-style arrangers do (because of the greater quantity of plant material used) using putty-type Oasis fix. (*See* MECHANICS)

PIN STRAIGHTENER

The kenzan-naoshi, or pin straightener, is more often found on ikebana sales' tables than western ones. It is an extremely useful little metal tube, not more than 5 cm (2 in.), for cleaning and straightening the points on a pinholder which do, after a while, get bent over.

PLANT MATERIAL

This somewhat cumbersome phrase is the only one, it seems, that can be found to cover all vegetable matter. 'Flora', used as the botanical term, would be accurate (and shorter), but most people still think of it as just 'flowers'. So 'plant material' it is, in spite of Henry Mitchell, gardening correspondent of *The Washington Post*, having described it as, 'one of the supremely vulgar phrases of our language'.

The umbrella phrase usually refers to cut material, but includes all flowers, buds, leaves, bracts, fruits, berries, vegetables, cones, seedheads, fungi, lichen and rooted plants.

All these are *natural* plant material, the word 'natural' being used to differentiate between things that have actually grown and those which are man-made and therefore **'artificial'** (q.v.), such as paper flowers, wax fruits or plastic leaves.

Natural plant material can appear in a number of guises: fresh, dried, preserved, skeletonized, dyed, painted, bleached or glittered. In Britain, it is also considered to include basketry cane and flowers or fantasy plant forms that have been made-up *from* natural plant materials (*see* **MADE-UP FLOWERS**). The addition of wires, glue and tape are usually acceptable in show work, but this is not so in all countries and many do not accept painted, dyed or glittered plant materials unless a show schedule specifically permits it. If in doubt, whether as competitor or judge, always check with the show organizers.

Plant material is the flower arranger's medium, as paint is to the artist or stone to the sculptor. Even within the limits of a small garden or balcony of houseplants, there is a surprising variety of plants that can be grown for cutting, and many arrangers could be far more adventurous and selective in what they grow, even though they are not gardeners first and foremost. (*See* FOLIAGE)

PLAQUE

In general the word means an ornamental tablet. In flower arrangement it has come to be accepted as a design in plant material, fresh or dried, which is assembled and displayed on a visible background, unlike a swag, where no background shows and it is merely part of the mechanics.

In competition rulings the plaque has suffered some confusing changes in the *NAFAS Handbook of Schedule Definitions*, being first considered synonymous with collage (which it is if dried/preserved materials are glued to a background, but not if fresh plant materials are arranged in floral foam

Plaque *A plaque of dried and preserved materials interpreting 'Flowers and the Theatre' by Elizabeth Tomkinson.*

secured to a base or background). There have been confusions over whether or not a plaque is framed and whether or not it has glass over it. The most recent definition (1988) includes plaques with pictures, saying they are assembled on a backing (although there is no mention of whether it needs to show) and that they may be framed or unframed, glazed or unglazed.

PLATE (TRAY or MOSS) GARDEN

The charm of small plate or tray gardens has been neglected of late. They have a long history, deriving from the Japanese 'bankei' miniature landscapes with figures, bridges and buildings. These gardens tend to be lumped in the children's classes at village shows, but have much to recommend them as decorations in the home. While they can be made at any time of the year, it is in spring, when small, short-stemmed flowers are available, that they are most delightful.

Use a deep dish, tray or very shallow bowl and put 1 cm ($\frac{1}{2}$ in.) layer of sand, peat or earth as a base. Cover this with moss of any kind, landscaping the area with a stone or two, or small pieces of driftwood. If you decide to use a branch of catkins, pussy willow or newly bursting leaf buds for a 'tree' you need a small pinholder, underneath the moss, to fix it on. Otherwise short-stemmed primroses, violets, grape hyacinths, polyanthuses, bluebells, daisies, forget-me-nots or rockery plants can be put straight into the moss in a hole made first with a skewer. Groups of flowers can be in a cut-off cigar tube of water concealed in the moss. Small figures can be added if you have them.

As with any **landscape** (q.v.) scale is the important factor. Any flower or leaf that is too large destroys the illusion.

Keep the base and moss moist, but not saturated, and mist-spray the garden from time to time. As flowers and leaves fade it takes only a moment to refresh the whole garden and in this way it will last for a month at least.

POINT

Arrangers became confused about the use of the word 'point' in the early 1970s. Until about that time the word had been used in two ways: first, in the term 'focal point' to mean the centre of interest of a flower arrangement; and secondly to describe plant material which came to a point, such as stems or branches ending in a bud, or tapering blade leaves. This 'pointed' plant material was likely to be the framework of a traditional massed design. The fully open flowers and larger leaves at the centre of a design were called 'rounds'.

Then came the move to use the word 'point' as printers and designers do. To the printer a 'full point' is what laymen call a 'full stop'. It is round, it arrests movement and holds the eye. It implies focal point but not tapering point. Gradually, then, the usage has changed, especially as it became fashionable to talk about 'centres of interest' in a design or arrangement, to steer beginners away from the 'bullseye' idea of just one big flower being used at the centre. Compare the old with the new terminology:

Then	Now
focal point	= centre of interest/focal area
rounds	= points
points/pointed material	= outline material

'Points' are not necessarily circular, and may be square or irregular, but they will not be elongated in any way or they begin to have direction outwards, not inwards. Points may be solid (a full open flower or an apple) or a more or less circular space enclosed by vines, cane, driftwood.

POLYTHENE
Because polythene is water-proof and very light in weight it is invaluable to the arranger in many ways.

Thick: either black, coloured or transparent for table coverings to work on or as a drop-sheet on the floor to protect it and to collect rubbish in.

Thin: use really thin polythene such as clingfilm or dry cleaner's bags for making 'sausages' for **garlands** (q.v.); and for covering wet floral foam to prevent it drying out too quickly. Unless a very thin type of polythene is used, it is difficult to insert softer flower and leaf stems, without using a skewer to make holes first, and that does slow down the process very considerably. Polythene can also be used for lining flower boxes to transport fresh flowers.

Bags: all conditioned foliage (except grey-leaved, which gets too moist and loses its greyness) can be stored for quite long periods in polythene bags sealed with a wire twist leaving a cushion of air inside. Leaves are readily transportable this way. It is better not to use too thick a bag which could damage them. Bags of any type are invaluable for collecting rubbish in churches, stately homes, hospitals, halls or classrooms, where rubbish disposal may not be available nearby, or where debris has to be taken home.

'Bubble' plastic: an excellent lightweight packaging material, useful for wrapping containers and accessories. Buy at hardware shops or garden centres.

POMANDER
There are really two kinds of pomander, though each accords with the description of 'a mixture of aromatic substances to be carried about with one, especially as a safeguard against infection' One is a hollow ball or filigree case made of gold, silver, ivory, or nowadays more often of perforated china, which holds a **pot pourri** (q.v.) of herbs and spices. The second is an orange, lemon, or more occasionally, an apple, stuck all over with cloves, and sometimes called a 'clove orange'.

To make a 'clove orange' pomander
- a medium-sized, thin-skinned orange
- about 50 gm (2 oz) cloves
- one short stub wire and a few rose wires (or fuse wire)
- 2 metres (yards) narrow ribbon 1 cm ($\frac{1}{2}$ in.) wide, odd pearl beads, sequins, gilded plastic leaves, etc.
- skewer and pliers

1 Mark out with a Biro where the ribbons will lie to 'quarter' the orange.
2 After making a hole with a skewer push the stub wire through from top to bottom of the orange and, using the pliers, bend over a small loop at each end.

Pomander *A 'clove orange' or pomander decorated with beads, ribbons and a long loop for hanging.*

Posy *A Victorian-style posy finished with a doily and ribbon bow.*

3 Push in cloves, touching each other, all over the orange, but leaving the ribbon channels free.

4 Leave, if possible, for a couple of days to start drying out.

5 Tie the ribbon round the orange going through the wire loops for extra security. Make a ribbon loop for hanging.

6 Decorate with wired beads, leaves, etc. and extra bows of ribbon if wished.

Gradually the pomander dries out until it is quite hard and light in weight, but the tangy clove smell lasts for a long time. Since few of us carry them about to ward off infection nowadays, they are hung in rooms or wardrobes and make pleasing small gifts, especially at Christmas, or for a patient in hospital.

POSY

A posy is variously described as a nosegay, a small bouquet or a bunch of flowers. It is descended from the *tussie-mussie* carried in mediaeval and Tudor times to bury one's nose in against noxious smells and as protection against the plague. It is, therefore, intended to be carried, and today's posy, which evolved in the nineteenth century, is circular and about 23 cm (9 in.) in diameter. Most are domed in the centre (like an inverted basin) and are finished off at the edge with a frill or doily of paper, net, tulle or lace, or a ring of leaves. The stems are brought together to form a handle which is bound with foil or ribbon, possibly with a bow and 'tails'.

The Royal Maundy posies carried by The Queen and Royal Almonry officials are made of spring flowers grouped in little bunches with cupressus, thyme and rosemary foliage. Each posy is made up of about 100 small flowers.

There are posies to suit all occasions: weddings, presentations, gifts to hospital patients and period styles. For competitive show work they are generally included in floristry schedules, rather than flower arrangement as such, because stems are usually wired (except for hospital gifts). The Victorian Judges' School for Floral Art in Australia which includes 'wired work', is specific about the Victorian style posy: it is described as 'slightly domed with concentric circles of flowers, approximately 15 cm (6 in.) in diameter, finished with a frill or paper doily and ribbon streamers'. They also define an 1830 posy as having 'one cone-shaped flower protruding from the centre'. For this style the concentric rings of flowers are compulsory and the outer edge must be finished with leaves only.

Spice posies have become very popular. They are made in the same way and include nutmegs, curls of cinnamon, peppercorns, pieces of ginger, poppy seedheads, beech mast, almonds, etc., all on wired stems.

Posyholders

In the nineteenth century cone-shaped posy holders became fashionable. Made of gold filigree, silver, ivory, amber, mother-of-pearl and often enamelled or bejewelled, they are collector's pieces today.

POT-ET-FLEUR

Pot-et-fleur (the term seems to be both singular and plural) was the name invented by *The Daily Telegraph* readers in 1960, following an article by Violet Stevenson on mixing cut flowers with what were then called 'pot plants', but now are almost invariably referred to as houseplants.

The plants are the mainstay of a pot-et-fleur and may be grouped in their pots in one larger container (method 1); or de-potted and planted in a large container in peat-based compost, or packed in sphagnum moss (method 2).

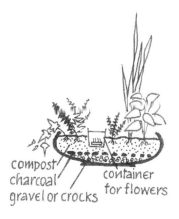

compost
charcoal
gravel or crocks

container
for flowers

Pot-et-fleur *A well-balanced pot-et-fleur, and construction details.*

Pot-et-fleur *A pot-et-fleur by Colette Archer, Preston (Brighton) Flower Club, on a tree trunk stand which was part of the staging provided (after the hurricane of 1987!).*

Method 1

The disadvantage is that an extra large container is needed to accommodate the pots and unless enough height can be made with the plants, the pot-et-fleur looks bottom-heavy. On the other hand it is easy to change plants if one looks wrong, gets too big or simply looks sickly. Nor is there the same need, as in method 2, of having plants that enjoy the same soil and watering conditions, for they can be given individual treatment. Drainage is easy because there will be plenty of spaces to help this.

Method 2
This is perhaps neater and tidier once the bowl has been planted. Take special care with the drainage and choose plants that are compatible in their soil and water needs. Insert one or two small containers for cut flowers when planting up the bowl.

Containers
The container must be deep enough to take the plant roots comfortably and leave room for watering. It must hold water with no drainage hole. A large bulb bowl, Victorian bedroom wash bowl, copper or brass preserving pan, plastic urn or a basket lined with heavy-duty polythene, are all suitable.

Arrangement
Apart from cultural compatability, choose plants which have a colour link and provide different heights, forms and textures. For example, in a bowl of five plants (five is about right, depending on the size of the container), choose one tall plant, one bushy, one fern-like, one trailing and one bold-leaved. They should be arranged to be pleasing and decorative even without the addition of flowers. Have at least one plant trailing over the rim of the container to break the hard line.

Flowers
To keep the emphasis on the plants, don't use too many flowers. There are no rules, though odd numbers are generally easier to arrange, so three to seven flowers are often enough for a domestic pot-et-fleur. Again, look for a colour to pick up from the leaves, if you can, and if one of the plants is flowering (and there is no reason why it should not be) then the two sorts of flowers should not clash.

Depending on the flowers used they will need to be stripped of most of their own leaves to avoid muddle. They can all be in one container (with a pinholder or floral foam as seems best) or in separate cigar or tablet tubes which are easily pushed down and hidden. But remember they need regular topping up. Driftwood, stones, a figurine and other accessories can be added if wished.

Pot-et-fleur never seem to have enjoyed the popularity they deserve among flower arrangers. A well-planted one can last for two to three years, and is not demanding of constant attention. It is always surprising they are not used more in churches (q v), especially in the winter months.

POT POURRI
Pot pourri, a mixture of dried petals, leaves, herbs and spices, has been used for centuries to perfume rooms. The chief ingredient is usually rose petals, but anything that still has an attractive aroma when dry can be used, and some can be added just for colour.

If possible, use the best-coloured, sweetest-smelling rose petals, lavender flowers, leaves of lemon verbena, marjoram, thyme and pineapple sage, delphiniums, pinks, camomile, marigolds and bergamot. Gather on a dry day and spread them out on trays or sheets of newspaper to dry in a warm airy place but out of strong light. Turn them gently once or twice during drying, which should only take a few days. When everything feels papery the ingredients are ready for 'fixing' with an essential oil. The traditional ones are orris root and gum benzoin, but you can buy sandalwood, bergamot, rosemary, rose geranium and others at chemists and herbal shops. Mix approximately one part herbs and spices to four parts of petals, sprinkle them with a half a dozen drops of oil and store in a covered container (plastic ice cream boxes are useful) for about a week, then the pot pourri is ready for use. Over time you will find what proportions of petals to herbs suit you and which oils you prefer.

In the eighteenth century porcelain pot pourri holders were made with perforated covers to allow the perfume to percolate into the room. Open bowls will lose their perfume more quickly, but it can be revived with a few drops of essential oil or with a commercial pot-pourri refresher.

(*See* **POMANDER**)

PRESERVING *see* **DRYING**

PRESSING *see* **DRYING**

PROPORTION (and SCALE)

Proportion and scale are two of the **design principles** (q.v.). Although two words are often interchanged, the meaning is clear.

Scale is about *size* relationships and for that reason is especially important in landscape, miniature and petite designs where, if anything is out of scale it looks incongruous, and in a landscape, destroys the illusion of a re-created scene. When several accessories are used in one design they must have the size relationship we are accustomed to, otherwise we reject them. A bird almost full size in the same scene as a tiny fox or human figure makes both look ridiculous.

Proportion is the relation of one part of a design to another part, or to the whole. It is more concerned with quantities, measurements and areas. The **Golden Section** (q.v.) deals with proportions and the division of a line or area which is felt to be most pleasing to the greatest number of people. This is also sometimes expressed as a mathematical series, as 2 is to 3, so 3 is to 5, 5 to 8, 8 to 13, and so on. It is from these concepts that flower arrangers took their rule of thumb for measurements: making the tallest stem one and a half times the greatest measurement of the container; placing an asymmetrical arrangement two-thirds of the way along a base; and making show niches 60 cm (2 ft) wide by 90 cm (3 ft) high.

RECESSION

Recession here means 'setting back'. In a massed arrangement some stems must be cut shorter to allow flowers and leaves to be behind others – not crowding them, but giving greater depth. An arrangement without some recession will look stalky and all the flowers will be in the same plane so that the front looks 'flat'. On the other hand, if *too* many flowers are recessed the arrangement begins to look 'stuffed' because all the space within the design is lost.

RENAISSANCE, ITALIAN (1400-1600)

Renaissance, the French word for 're-birth', is the name given to the period following the Middle Ages, when Europe, and Italy in particular, experienced a great revival of the arts, science and learning. Based on the classical concepts of Ancient **Greece and Rome** (q.v.) the Renaissance developed the humanistic belief in the importance and dignity of Man. Trade with the east brought prosperity to Europe and wealthy, powerful, families became lavish patrons of the arts and built and furnished splendid palaces.

Renaissance, Italian *Details from Italian Renaissance paintings (1400–1600).*

Although the emphasis had shifted from art purely for the glorification of God, and there was much civil and secular work, it is in the Renaissance altarpieces that most of the evidence of the use of flowers is found. Flowers 'stood in attendance on Christ' almost always with a symbolic, religious message to the mass of people who could not read or write.

Settings

After the dark, cloistered Middle Ages, the emphasis was on light and space with perspective views through rounded archways to gardens or landscapes beyond; classical columns; frescoes on walls and ceilings; floors of coloured marble or terracotta tiles; large elaborate fireplaces in marble or stone; balustrades; brick buildings faced with marble; gilt painted gesso furniture; richly carved wooden chests and wardrobes; oriental carpets; Genoese velvet; damasks and brocades often with metallic threads.

Flowers and plants

The flower featured above all others in Renaissance paintings is the Madonna lily, *Lilium candidum*, symbolic of purity and chastity. Next is the rose, red, pink and white (usually the centifolia type, shown fully open), but occasionally the single white rose for simplicity. The pink, or small carnation, is featured too, often as a pot plant growing indoors, carefully staked. The aquilegia (columbine) appears, symbolizing the gifts of the Holy Spirit; the violet is for humility and the daisy for innocence. The blue iris stands for majesty and Mary as the Queen of Heaven, and the orange lily for Christ himself, as well as the crown imperial. In addition, there are all the flowers featured in the *millefiori* tapestries and paintings of flower-scattered meadows, as in Botticelli's *Primavera* (1482) which portrays some 500 individual plants, in more than 40 varieties. These include the buttercup, cornflower, (white campion *Lychnis alba*), corn marigold, forget-me-not, dandelion, hellebore, jasmine, crocus and flax. Foliage included myrtle, leaves of the citrus trees, cupressus, acanthus, arum, bay, laurel, oak, olive, pine, ivy, vine, box and most herbs. Clipped topiary trees were seen indoors and out. The most important fruits were those of the citrus trees, pomegranate, grapes, melon and peach. Apples, cherries, figs, pears, plums and quinces were known and, among the vegetables, the artichoke and cucumber.

Containers

Decanter-like or tumbler-shaped clear glass vases, low woven baskets; majolica ware; terracotta urns; or silver utensils, which are often shown displayed as a decorative feature at banquets.

Arrangements and uses

1 The garland is featured in several ways:
   (a) they are worn on the head and round the neck (as in Botticelli's *Primavera*) much as garlands are made today, on a basis of foliage, with flowers dotted through;
   (b) they are strung across the top of the picture behind or above the chief figure. Most are of foliage and fruits often held in cornucopia-like holders at either end. One shows 'balls' of wide-open roses strung along a rope like huge beads.
   (c) Della Robbia glazed ceramic panels feature circular or arched garlands of fruit, flowers and foliage.
2 Arrangements set at the feet of the Virgin in altarpieces, or being offered by attendant angels, are of roses or pinks in flat woven simple narrow-necked vases of glass or metal and sometimes in low, bulbous bowls.
3 Taller majolica ware vases, apothecaries' jars, metal or ceramic urns have mixed bunches of flowers and foliage, sometimes with one or two tall lilies towering above the rest.
4 Small, strewn flowers are seen on banqueting tablecloths.

Symbolism
The flowers in altarpieces are symbolic (see above, **Flowers and plants**) as are those in secular paintings. (*See* **PERIOD ARRANGING**)

RHYTHM

Rhythm is one of the **design principles** (q.v.). Arrangers often speak of 'flowing' designs and 'movement' within an arrangement and these are simply other ways of referring to rhythm. Without rhythm, an arrangement looks static and lifeless, no matter how lovely the flowers are.

Rhythm can be achieved in several ways:

1 by using 'line' plant material such as curving branches or stems; the eye naturally follows a line.
2 by repetition, whether of lines, shapes or colours. Just one of anything is eye-catching; two make the eye move from one to the other; three and the movement is extended; six or seven and the eye follows the repetition as surely as it would a solid line.
3 by radiation, or lines fanning out from a central point. They may not be as obvious as the spokes of a wheel or the ribs of a fan, but the effect of flowers and leaves emerging from one place, the container, creates rhythm.
4 by **transition** (q.v.) or gradation of shapes, sizes and colours, e.g., the familiar movement in an arrangement from small buds in the outline, to opening buds, half-open flowers, and fully-open flowers at the centre is transition both of shape and size; the use of pale pinks, through deeper pinks to red and then dark red is a gradation of one colour.
5 by lines of continuance, which are not tangible, but invisible 'lines' created by features sufficiently important to make the eye move from one to another in a rhythmic sweep over the design, e.g., in an arrangement using a figurine as an accessory, the eye will often move, as if by compulsion, from the figurine to the central, largest flowers and then up to the pointed tip of a design and back down to the figurine and so on.

RIBBONS

Cheap waterproof floristry ribbons, plain, textured, flocked or lacy, are available in a wide range of colours. Many flower club sales tables, florists and garden centres have a good stock. Whilst ribbon bows, loops and streamers look well with arrangements at Christmas, weddings and other festivals, they can detract from the flowers, so use them with discretion.

Ribbon made of polypropylene does not fray and will tear lengthwise into narrow strips, unlike woven ribbon.

ribbon folded
into three lengths
to make
figure-of-
eight bow

tail single loop

Ribbons *Florist ribbon does not tie easily. Mount each part of a bow separately on wire. A double or triple loop can be made in the same way.*

Square ends look clumsy; cut ends on a slant or in a fish tail.

A whole length, or just the ends, can be curled if you hold the ribbon firmly in your left hand and pull it over the back of a knife with the right hand. The sharper and firmer the pull, the tighter the curl. To straighten, do the same on the other side of the ribbon.

Ribbons from haberdashery counters are generally more expensive and, although most of them today are of man-made fibres, they do have a softness and draping quality which florist ribbons do not. But they don't stand up nearly so well outdoors in the rain!

ROCOCO, FRENCH (1715–1774)

Strictly, rococo is a style, not a period, but it has been taken to describe French arranging of the eighteenth century. The word derives from *rocailles* (rocks) and *coquilles* (shells) and describes a style essentially asymmetrical, free-flowing and full of 'S' and 'C' curves. It followed the heavier baroque style of the seventeenth century and, originating in France, influenced art and decor in almost every European country, especially Austria and Germany. Patronage of the arts by the powerful mistresses of the French kings produced masterpieces of porcelain, tapestries, fabrics and paintings.

Settings

In common with **Renaissance** (q.v.) settings, emphasis is on light, flowing in through windows and French doors and reflected in mirrors and glass chandeliers; elegant furniture in light woods inlaid with marquetry and porcelain plaques and medallions; carved and gilded wood and stucco decorations with garlands, bows and curving acanthus swirls; Gobelin tapestries with natural and mythological scenes, garlands, swags and baskets of flowers; Sèvres porcelain; paintings of pastoral scenes; chinoiserie; silk, satin and *Toile de Jouy* fabrics.

Colours

Clear pastel colours such as shell pink, turquoise, apricot, warm grey with accents of darker blue and violet; pale blue ribbons; gold everywhere.

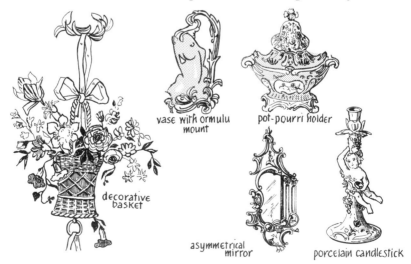

vase with ormulu mount

pot-pourri holder

decorative basket

asymmetrical mirror

porcelain candlestick

Rococo, French *Curls and swirls typical of French Rococo (1715–1774).*

Plant materials

Full-blown roses, lilac, peonies and the guelder rose (*Viburnum opulus sterile*) seem especially typical of the period with larkspur, poppies, tulips and antirrhinums and gladioli recently introduced. Little foliage is added. Fruit included the pineapple, orange, peach, nectarine, apricot, grapes and strawberries grown in the orangeries or hot-houses; apples, pears, cherries and quinces were grown out-of-doors.

Containers

Porcelain urns, handled and footed, often on their own plinth; marble and alabaster vases; celadon vases with ormolu mounts; and tall flare-topped baskets.

Arrangements and uses

Flowers in vases and urns have all the movement of the later Dutch/Flemish massed designs, but are a little lighter and more open and colourings more pastel.

Garlands and swags in tapestries are rich and full, mainly of summer flowers. The effect is always of high summer with full-blown flowers and curving stems; the flowers seeming to spill from their containers and garlands often continue the line.

Dining and banqueting tables seem primarily to have been decorated with epergnes and ornaments and sugar confectionery scenes. Pyramids of fruit stood on tazzas (saucer-shaped dishes mounted on feet) down the length of the table.

Accessories and symbolism

Practically no accessories are seen with the flowers and there is no evidence of symbolism. (*See* **PERIOD ARRANGING**)

ROMAN *see* **GREEK** *and* **ROMAN**

ROYAL HORTICULTURAL SOCIETY (RHS)

The RHS, formed in 1804 (it became 'Royal' in 1861), is a society of both amateur gardeners and professional horticulturists. Anyone with an interest in gardening may become a member, and will receive the monthly journal *The Garden* and the newsletter giving details of activities, shows, lectures, etc.

The Society maintains 250 acres of gardens at Wisley in Surrey, which are designed to show members what they can grow or achieve in their own gardens. The RHS organizes the famous Chelsea Flower Show, held each year in May, in the grounds of the Royal Hospital in Chelsea, the home of the red-coated 'Chelsea Pensioners' in London.

At the London headquarters of the Society there are two large exhibition halls where shows are held throughout the year. The RHS Lindley Library, the most important of its kind in the world, houses some 36,000 books.

See **APPENDIX: ADDRESSES**

SAW

It is useful to have a small saw in the flower arranger's toolbox and a folding pruning saw about 20 cm (8 in.) long, when the blade is folded into the handle, is an excellent all-purpose saw for driftwood, branches etc. More ingenious and inexpensive is the boy scout's pocket saw available where camping equipment is sold. A cutting wire about 45 cm (18 in.) long has a metal ring at either end, and the saw is pulled back and forth with two hands.

SCALE *see* PROPORTION

SCHEDULE

American arrangers call the schedule 'the law of the show', and any show schedule should be a well-prepared leaflet/booklet, attractive to would-be exhibitors, giving full details of date(s), venue, time of opening, staging and dismantling, eligibility for entry, closing date(s) and fees for entries and the name and address of the show secretary. It will also give details of the classes and their requirements and all the rules and regulations governing the show.

Intending exhibitors must read this carefully. It is important. If anything is not clear or not understood the show secretary should be consulted. If necessary, he or she will consult the appointed judge(s) who will normally have approved the draft schedule before printing. Schedule wording can sometimes be ambiguous, so if in doubt, *ask*.

Many schedules state that judging will be in accordance with a handbook of definitions, a glossary of show terms, or a show guide or manual. It is important, if you are competing, to obtain and refer to this booklet as well. In Britain most flower arrangement shows are judged 'in accordance with the *NAFAS Handbook of Schedule Definitions*' though there are other rules published by the **RHS** (q.v.), the Women's Institute and other organizations. The handbook is revised every five years or so, and it is important to consult an up-to-date copy. Again, if in doubt, consult the show secretary.

At smaller shows the schedule often doubles as the show programme or brochure to save the extra cost of printing a separate one. It is important, therefore, to make it as attractive, and as clear as possible, so that everyone seeing the show will be well informed.

The definition for flower arrangement classes in horticultural shows used to be, 'a vase of flowers arranged for effect' or 'a bowl of mixed garden flowers', which identified these 'decorative classes' (as they were, and often still are, known) from the horticultural exhibits. Since about 1950, flower arrangement shows and individual classes have tended to have titles, and each entrant is expected to interpret this title. (*See* **INTERPRETATION**)

For each flower arrangement class a schedule should give all the information needed on these lines:

Title	Description	Dimensions	Staging	Other Information
Suddenly it's spring	A landscape exhibit. Fresh plant material	75 cm wide × 90 cm high × 60 cm deep	In a niche painted blue-grey with side wings 25 cm deep, on tabling 70 cm from floor, covered in blue-grey fabric	Open to novice club members only
A night at the opera	An interpretative exhibit. Title of opera to be stated	120 cm diameter Height unlimited	On a round platform 30 cm high covered in natural hessian	May be staged by up to three exhibitors

SCHEDULE DEFINITIONS, NAFAS HANDBOOK OF

This is the NAFAS booklet of rules and glossary of terms used in competitive show work, obtainable from NAFAS (*see* **APPENDIX ADDRESSES**). The very first version was a stencilled sheet in 1958 and it is now updated about every five years. It is interesting that reference to class titles and their interpretation does not appear until the fourth edition in 1967. If you are a show competitor, don't leave home without it and be sure it is up-to-date. Use it in conjunction with the *NAFAS Judges Manual* for greater detail and guidance.

Most other countries with flower arrangement organizations have similar publications, e.g., *Handbook for Flower Shows* (America), *Handbook and Show Guide* (Natal), *Floral Art Handbook* (New Zealand) and *Definition et Reglement pour Concours Floraux* published by the Belgian Flower Arrangement Society in association with flower arrangement organizations in Spain, Monaco, Holland, Italy and France. If competing abroad be sure to check which rules are in force.

SCISSORS, FLOWER

Flower scissors are normally about 15 cm (6 in.) long with stubby, round-ended blades, one at least serrated and a notch for cutting fine wires. They will cut flower stems and slender woody stems. **Secateurs** (q.v.) are needed for thicker branches.

Cutters for **ikebana** (q.v.) known as 'hasami' are rather different, having no finger and thumb holds and are held in the palm between the thumb and all the fingers.

SECATEURS

Many arrangers prefer secateurs to **scissors** (q.v.) for all cutting tasks in flower arranging, but they are certainly needed for thick, woody stems. Slim, pointed straight-edged secateurs, often called trimmers, will cut through wood up to finger thickness yet are fine enough for more detailed work and serve as an all-purpose cutter.

For heavier duty with branches, larger secateurs will be needed and it is
very much a personal choice whether to have straight or curved blades.

SEED COLLAGE

The sheer range and variety of seeds available makes this type of collage
attractive, though seed cases and some preserved leaves are often included,
mainly for texture changes. Seeds vary in size, from tiny poppy seeds to large
peach stones; in shape, from the perfect sphere to the elongated ellipse; in
texture, from high shine to dull matt; and in colour through the rainbow
range, from translucent white rice, green peas, orange lentils, striped
hogweed, brown coriander, to glistening black hosta.

Sources

Household waste: apple, pear, orange, lemon and grape pips; peach, plum
and apricot stones; melon, pepper, tomato seeds, etc.

Grocers: spices of all sorts, rice, pulses, coffee beans, peppercorns.

Hedgerows: hogweed, dock, plantain, bluebell, poppy, rape, beech mast, ash
keys, broom.

Garden: hollyhock, hosta, iris, marigold, sisyrinchium, nigella, grasses,
artichoke, laburnum, parsnip.

Pet shop: millet, sunflower seeds, corn.

Every collagist has his/her favourite adhesive, some using Copydex, others
UHU (leaving any 'strings' to dry and then cutting them away) or clear
Bostick.

   Any subject can be chosen from landscapes to portraits, animals, birds,
flowers, heraldic devices or simply abstract patterns. (*See* picture, page 41)

SEEDHEADS

Seedheads add much interest to a mixed flower arrangement at almost any
time of the year, but are especially useful in autumn and winter, combined
with dried and glycerined material.

   While all seedheads will dry on the plant, for the best results harvest them
when they have matured, but before rain, wind and frost begin to damage
them. Tie in loose bunches and hang upside down to dry in a dry, airy place.

   Some of the seedheads most popular with flower arrangers include:

Acer (sycamore)	Crocosmia
Agapanthus	Digitalis (foxglove)
Allium (onion, all types)	*Dipsacus fullonum* (teasel)
Althaea (hollyhock)	Grasses (many kinds)
Angelica	Heracleum (hogweed)
Antirrhinum (better glycerined)	Iris (all types, including
Aquilegia (columbine)	*I. foetidissima* with orange berries)
Ballota	Lunaria (honesty – silver pennies)
Carpinus (hornbeam)	Nicandra
Centaurea	Nigella (love-in-a-mist)
Corn, ornamental	Papaver (poppy)

Physalis (Chinese lantern or
    Cape gooseberry)
Reedmace (bulrush)
Rumex (dock)

Scabiosa 'Paper Moon'
Sisyrinchium
Verbascum (mullein)
Yucca gloriosa

Unusual (and often unnamed) seedheads, imported from overseas, are on
sale at garden centres and florists. When buying, look for unusual shapes or
different textures to augment those from the garden.

Many seedheads can be used in arrangements at the 'green' stage and will
begin to dry out. When the arrangement is done with, they can be bunched
and hung up to finish drying. If arranged with fresh materials in water or
damp foam, varnish the stem ends or bind them with clear adhesive tape to
prevent mildew.

SEEING EYE

Much has been said about the flower arranger's 'seeing eye', and flower
arranging has indeed opened the eyes of many a newcomer to the hobby
like the new student at a course of springtime lessons who exclaimed
delightedly that she had found spotted arum leaves growing by her dustbin!
They had probably been growing there for years, but it was not until flower
arranging entered her life that she really 'saw' them, and their spots.

One revelation like this and the world becomes a more fascinating place.
In nature there is subtle colour to appreciate, texture of bark or leaves to
discover, the huge range of greens in foliage to marvel at and the shapes of
things to relate to other things. Indoors there is a new perception of colour
schemes, of spaces, of fabrics, of woods. In junk shops and rubbish heaps
there are treasures to be hunted for likely containers or accessories. On the
seashore there are shells and driftwood. In libraries there are books with
pictures; in museums and stately homes there are paintings, sculptures,
architecture, furniture, carving and a host of other arts and crafts to admire.
Life is never the same again. Once the eye is opened it never really closes,
except for reflection. Planning and sorting out how a new find might be used
is a necessary part of the 'seeing'. As George Roualt described it, 'that I might
better see the vision bloom and submit itself to orderly arrangement.'

The flower arranger is not alone in this perception, for every artist, in
whatever medium, develops a seeing eye. But very few are blessed with such
a varied a medium as Nature provides, so there is never an end to the
'seeing'.

SHAKESPEARE'S FLOWERS

Shakespeare, born a countryman, mentions by name over 100 wild flowers,
trees, herbs and fruits in his plays and poems. A most comprehensive little
reference book is *The World of Shakespeare: Plants* by Alan Dent (*see*
APPENDIX: BOOKS).

SHELLS

Shells, another product of Nature, have an affinity with flowers and their
mother-of-pearl sheen can inspire pastel-coloured arrangements. Large
shells can be used as containers and smaller seashore finds for miniatures
and petites. The **Victorians** (q.v.) grew pot plants in large shells, drilled to

hang by three cords. Covering jars and bowls with small shells glued on or set in a cement to make decorated flower containers or boxes for trinkets was another Victorian handicraft.

Making up flowers out of shells, either for pictures or three-dimensional arrangements, to stand under glass domes or in glass cases, was popular in the eighteenth and nineteenth centuries, and examples of this skill and artistry can be seen in many museums and stately homes. Present-day three-dimensional **collages** (q.v.) of shell-flowers often have a card backing on which individual flowers are composed before being added to the design.

Shells used as accessories in seascapes look best if grouped in only one or two places, as opposed to being scattered all over the base.

SHOWS

Shows are an opportunity for an arranger to display his/her talents to a greater public than the family and friends at home. In Britain, most flower arrangement shows (as opposed to festivals in churches or stately homes) are competitive, following horticultural society practice. Although not every arranger likes the idea of competition or of interpreting a title with an arrangement, a competitive show is an excellent exercise and any arranger wanting to progress, to teach, judge or demonstrate flower arrangement really must serve an apprenticeship at shows. It is the discipline and the chance to measure one's own ability against others that is invaluable.

There are two aspects to every show: organizing and competing.

Shows *An overall view of the NAFAS festival 'Flight of Fancy' on the preview evening at the Brighton Centre.*

The show scene

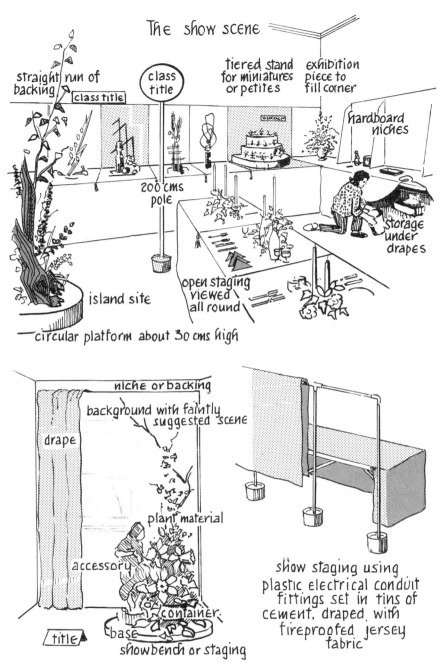

straight run of backing

class title

class title

tiered stand for miniatures or petites

exhibition piece to fill corner

hardboard niches

200 cms pole

storage under drapes

island site

open staging viewed all round

circular platform about 30 cms high

niche or backing

background with faintly suggested scene

drape

plant material

accessory

container

title

base

showbench or staging

show staging using plastic electrical conduit fittings set in tins of cement, draped with fireproofed jersey fabric

components of a show exhibit

Organizing a club/village show

1 Choose a date carefully, with holidays and other local events in mind. Book a hall, usually for the day, plus half a day or the evening, before.
2 Select a committee and allocate jobs which should include:
   Chairman – to think ahead, enthuse, cajole, inspire and hold all the strings together.
   Secretary – to deal with correspondence, schedules, entries, show cards, prizes, trophies.
   Treasurer – to handle all monies, pay bills, insurance, bank receipts and provide floats for stalls on the day.
   Design and staging manager – to supervise layout of hall, allocation of spaces, tabling, covers, backing or niches, class titles, exhibition pieces, water supply, rubbish.
   Publicity – (within and outside the organization) to deal with press.
   Sales tables – to provide extra stock and helpers.
   Fund raising – to manage the raffle or tombola.
   Hospitality – to provide teas for the public and refreshments for committee, stall-holders and judge.
3 Book a judge and show opener if one is needed.
4 Give the show a title and get the schedule out as soon as possible. It is usually compiled by a small sub-committee with at least one experienced schedule-maker on it and should be checked by the judge.
5 Publicity is vital to the success of any show and often a largely neglected item. If your advert is in a shop or building it might be part of an actual arrangement. Consider these possibilities:

Ways of advertising	*Publicity spots*
posters and handbills	library
local press	information centre
flower arranging magazines	community centre
local radio	local shops
local clubs – Women's	local florists
Institute, Townswomen's	garden centres
Guild, horticultural society,	building societies
church groups, etc.	banks
sandwich boards on day	newsagents
newsy items in advance to local	fences, gates, trees, doors of
press	members and friends

Setting up the show

Much depends on what space is available and how many classes have to be fitted in (don't overdo it and have everything squashed up) but aim at an open look as visitors enter the hall. The plan should be worked out *in detail* on graph paper well in advance, and sufficient trestles or folding tables ensured.

There are two ways of providing simple but effective settings for each exhibit:
1 Cover all the tables with man-made fibre jersey fabric, which is virtually uncrushable, bringing the covering down to 2 cm ($\frac{3}{4}$ in.) from the floor (not touching) so that it hangs well. Cream, beige, mushroom, grey-green or grey-blue all set off exhibits well. Lay transparent polythene sheeting on the table tops.

To provide a backing, use the same fabric draped over a framework made from lightweight plastic tubing sold, with joints, for electrical conduits. (See diagram on page 151.) The uprights should stand in tins filled with cement for stability.

2 The alternative is to use free-standing **niches** (q.v.) of plywood, hardboard or thick cardboard, painted to tone with the fabric table covering. These will pack flat and store easily.

Island sites, either square or round, for group or large exhibits, can simply be marked out on the floor, or low platforms can be provided if the club can go to that expense. Throw-over fabric squares or circles are adequate covers for these.

Miniatures look much better on a raised stand, preferably at eye-level, and a handyman can help here.

Mark out exhibitors' spaces with tapes or chalk which can be removed *after* judging.

Have class titles up high, preferably over 2 metres (6 ft).

Entering and competing

If your flower club has competitions at its monthly meetings, start there and note the comments of the person who judges or assesses the exhibits. Talk to him/her if the chance arises. One learns much by mistakes and helpful criticism. If there is no club competition, or when you feel ready, enter the local club or horticultural society show.

1 Acquire a **schedule** (q.v.) and read it carefully. Note the date(s) and times of staging and be sure you can be free.

2 Enter a beginners or novice class if there is one, because competition there will be easier. If another class especially appeals, enter that as well if you wish, but tackle no more than two classes at your first show.

3 Be sure you understand (a) the class details, (b) the regulations and (c) any reference to other rules affecting the judging, such as the *NAFAS Handbook of Schedule Definitions*. If you don't understand, ask the show secretary.

4 Make sure your entry is made, accepted, and due fees paid well before closing date.

5 Begin to do the homework on your chosen class(es). See **INTERPRET-ATION** and **JUDGING** so that you know what you're aiming at.

6 When the show is about a week or so away, have a mock-up in a space or against a wall, marked out with the size allocated in the schedule. Don't guess; accuracy matters. Plan the exhibit well inside that space but make good use of it. A judge will penalize an exhibit for being too small in height, width or depth, but will have to disqualify it if it is too large (*see* **NOT ACCORDING TO SCHEDULE**).

7 Order flowers if necessary, prepare container, base, mechanics etc. as needed. Make a check list of all you will need to take to the show.

8 On the day (or the night before) put everything ready and mark each item off against your check list. Don't clutter yourself with too much; just take what plant material you will need plus a few spares. See that everything has your name on it. (*See* **PACKING**)

9 On arrival at the show, check in with the show secretary, find your allocated space(s) and put everything neatly nearby. Don't block gangways and don't encroach on neighbouring spaces or you will be very unpopular!

10 Set to work quietly and composedly. Keep calm by taking several deep breaths and settle down to *enjoy* the arranging.
11 After a while go away and look at your exhibit from a distance. You can assess it better from there.
12 Finish off, tidy up, top up with water and spray if you can do so without marking anything, then move away. Don't fiddle.
13 Have a break, a cup of coffee, a walk round taking care not to get in anyone's way, or to distract them, especially if staging time is running out.
14 Go back to the exhibit and make a final check: see the exhibitor's card is in place, blow or flick bits away, check for 'syphoning' from a leaf – and go home.

After judging: Going back to see the results is pure anguish. If you're a prize or award-winner, that's fine. If not, don't be discouraged, but appreciate what you've learned. Read the judge's comments, then read what has been said on other exhibits. Compare the prizewinners and learn from them. It will all be valuable next time you enter.

Tips for success
- It is not just the flower arrangement itself that the judge considers. How well the entire space allocated has been used is taken into consideration, and any base, background, accessory, title card and container as well as the plant material.
- Don't overdo the **accessories** (q.v.). Try to group them rather than dotting them about.
- Make each piece of plant material and each component do something in the design. If it doesn't, take it out. Most show exhibits tend to be too crowded.
- Attention to detail is the hallmark of any prizewinner. The hastily scribbled title card can ruin a potentially prize-winning exhibit.

(*See* **APPENDIX: BOOKS**)

SINGEING STEMS
Stems which exude a milky sap when cut are best treated by singeing in a flame before being put in water. They include poppies (papaver) and all spurges (euphorbia) including poinsettias. Hold the cut end in the flame (gas, match or candle) until it is blackened and no more liquid oozes out. (*See* **CONDITIONING**)

SKELETONIZING LEAVES
Skeletonized leaves (usually magnolia) can sometimes be bought, either natural in colour or dyed, but it is quite possible, with some patience, to do your own. Victorian ladies called them 'phantoms' and they were often used in dried arrangements under a glass dome or for flower pictures.

Choose tough, mature, but unmarked leaves such as camellia, magnolia, laurel or rhododendron. Boil the leaves for about an hour in a large saucepan with two good handfuls of washing soda. Test one leaf by trying to rub away the fleshy part under running water. Use rubber gloves. If unsuccessful, boil the leaves for longer and try again. When ready, it should be possible to scrape away gently all the fleshy tissue, leaving only a skeleton of veins. Deal with one leaf at a time, then soak it in diluted household bleach and spread it on kitchen paper or a newspaper to dry. The 'phantoms' can then be pressed for use in pictures or given a wire stem and gently curved or curled, in steam, for use in arrangements. They can be dyed with fabric dyes or sprayed with colour if wished. Store them separately from other materials as they tear easily.

SKEWERS

Wooden/kebab skewers are invaluable for spearing and anchoring fruit and vegetables in an arrangement. The food can then be eaten later.

Metal skewers are useful for making holes for soft-stemmed flowers and leaves in floral foam (wet or dry) and through polythene-wrapped floral foam for garlands, swags or plaques.

SPACE

Space is the least tangible of the **design elements** (q.v.). It is perhaps the most difficult quality for western arrangers to appreciate and to use, accustomed as they are to full massed designs. Space has always been understood, accepted, even venerated, by the East. As far back as the sixteenth century the Japanese were creating gardens with no plants, just rocks and raked sand.

Although space is important in a massed arrangement, enough at least for the form of each flower and leaf to be seen, it is in free-style and abstract designs that it is seen to advantage. The limited amount of plant material used means that space is inevitably part of the design and unless it is managed as well as the solid features, the result will not be good. An excellent exercise is to arrange a free-style design, then to draw within a defined rectangle the spaces created and shade or colour them in. The result is a 'negative' of the arrangement, and one can see where improvements of the shape or size of the spaces can be made. This is a useful exercise, but takes no account, of course, of the third dimension and has no depth. Similarly, a photograph shows no depth, which is why photos of flower arrangements can be disappointing because they look so cluttered. However, in a comparatively confined area, such as a show niche, space can be positively used and manipulated to give, or at least to suggest, more depth. Angling the exhibit diagonally within the niche gives greater depth at one side or the other, in front of, and behind, the arrangement. Leaving enough space on either side and at the top of the arrangement makes it look as if it fits, and reasonably fills the area allowed, but is not imprisoned by it. Lifting the container or base on feet or a stand creates a little space underneath the design.

Enclosed space

Free-style and modern arrangements emphasize this by using containers and driftwood with holes in them, and looped stems and leaves. Other enclosed spaces are visually created between two or three items used. The eye also tends to make a mental completion of the line between two points which are not actually joined but which indicate the bounds of a space area.

Space *Edith Brack's free-style study of spaces balanced by solid forms.*

Space around
Visually we are only able to appreciate the space around an arrangement if its background is plain. Any line, pattern or even a sharp-edged shadow behind becomes part of the design. Whilst we may know there is space to walk round an island site at a show we can only *see* it as part of what lies behind.

Space allowed
Show schedules are sometimes remiss in not stating clearly the height, width and depth of the space allocated for an exhibit. 'Space allowed 60cm × 60cm (2 ft × 2 ft)' is a common statement and the competitor is left wondering whether it means 60cm × 60cm (2 ft × 2 ft) on the table top or 60cm wide by 60cm high (2 ft wide by 2 ft deep), leaving the depth unstated. When in doubt *ask* the show secretary. From experience the phrase usually means 60cm wide by 60cm deep (2 ft wide by 2 ft deep) and the height is unstated, but it is never safe to assume this.

SPEAKER

A flower arrangement speaker will give talks on some specialist aspects of the art/craft such as pressed flower pictures, show work, period design, or foliage to grow. Clubs often have the idea that speakers just talk or lecture and there is nothing visual, but speakers for club meetings usually have plenty to show in the way of slides, examples of work, samples of plant material, books, pictures and charts.

SPLITTING STEMS

When preparing woody stems for **conditioning** (q.v.) split the ends with a knife or secateurs for about 2 cm ($\frac{3}{4}$ in.) to help them take up water more quickly through the wider cut area.

SPRAYING

Mist-spraying an arrangement of fresh flowers and foliage with water helps to keep moist the atmosphere around it and reduces the loss of water through transpiration. Use a small house-plant spray. It is specially beneficial in hot weather or in the dry atmosphere of central heating and air-conditioning. If spraying *in situ* protect polished surfaces and fabrics that may mark. (*See* **CONDITIONING**)

STABILE and STAMOBILE *see* MOBILE

STATELY HOMES

Flower festivals held in stately homes have been tremendously popular over the last 20 years or so in Britain. They have helped to raise millions of pounds for charity. This is no place to go into detail about the organization of such a festival (*see* **FLOWER FESTIVALS**) but to offer several points for designers and arrangers to keep in mind.

1 A festival is not, normally, intended to show a house and rooms decorated as they would be in daily use. It has to be larger than life or visitors will not feel they have had their money's worth. Nevertheless the flowers should accent, not overwhelm or obscure, the decorative features of the house, the furniture, paintings or other treasures. One sometimes has the impression that every horizontal surface has a flower arrangement on it. Discretion and selection are important.

2 A house can seldom be decorated entirely in the style of the period of its architecture and contents, but it should be possible, in certain rooms or parts of the house, to emulate that period style or to take certain characteristics from it and interpret them in contemporary fashion.

3 Visitors to a festival never find it easy to cope with looking at the guide-book, festival brochure *and* the exhibits all at once, especially if they are in a queue and have to keep putting on their reading spectacles! Designers and arrangers should guard against being carried away by their own knowledge and research. Interpretative exhibits of the history of the house or of famous people connected with it, should be self-explanatory whenever possible.

4 A viewing day is almost always set aside for arrangers to see the house, meet the designers and become familiar with their assignments. Make the most of it. Absorb the atmosphere of the house, buy the guidebook, take

copious notes, measurements and photographs if allowed, make sketches
and use paint colour cards for matching colours in the setting. You will
NOT remember all this accurately a few days later unless you have a
record for when you plan at home.

5 A big mistake is to assume that because a room is larger or more ornate
than you are used to, it will need more of everything. What it will need is
everything *larger*, to have sufficient impact.

Stately Homes *An elegant decoration of an elegant room, by Sevenoaks
Flower Club.*

STEM BINDING

Wire or wired stems are usually bound with tape before use in arrangements. The tape used to be of gutta-percha but is nowadays either plastic or
waxed crêpe paper. Both are 12 mm ($\frac{1}{2}$ in.) wide, available in rolls, in green,
brown and white.

Hold the stem to be taped in the left hand. Press the tape firmly once or
twice round the top where the stem joins the flower or leaf. Holding the tape
in the right hand, twirl the stem with the left bringing the tape down to cover
it in a spiral movement, each turn overlapping the previous one. Stretch the
tape slightly as you do this. Cut or tear the tape at the bottom and mould the
tape onto the stem with the fingers. It sounds complicated, but after a few
attempts it is easy to do very quickly.

For very fine stems mounted with silver rose wires, cut the tape into half
widths or less to keep the work as neat and fine as possible. (*See* **WIRING**)

STILL LIFE

In painting, a still life (Dutch – *stilleven*; French – *nature morte*) is a
representation of inanimate objects such as furniture, domestic utensils,

food and (surprisingly, perhaps, to flower arrangers) flowers and fruit. The well-known Dutch/Flemish flower-pieces are examples of still life in painting. For some painters a still life was an exercise to display their skills in portraying different textures, the roundness of objects, the highlights on glass or metal and the general play of light and shadow.

In flower arrangement the term is rather less clear. Although in Britain, still life has been an entry in *NAFAS Schedule Definitions* since 1982, it is not a show class that has been much used or explored. This is probably because NAFAS rules require plant material to predominate in ALL competitive show exhibits, and in still life that is something of a contradiction in terms, except where flower-pieces are concerned.

Still Life *A still life group of fruit, pottery and basketry. Real and artificial grapes are used and a spray of* Viburnum tinus.

Natal, New Zealand and America, to quote a few, stress that the *objects* rather than the plant material may predominate. The Americans go further in this. In her *Encyclopaedia of Judging and Exhibiting* Mrs E. V. Hame'l says that such a class is 'interpreted more by the objects, than by the choice or dominance of the plant materials, in contrast to an accessory which merely supplements the story.'

One thing everyone seems to agree about is that the objects included in a still life should be true to normal size (not small-scale models, say, as in a landscape scene) and true to function. Their choice should not be haphazard but related by a subject or theme of some kind, e.g., breakfast table, Victoriana, music, the sea, pottery, or by shape, colour or occasion. They should make an aesthetically pleasing group with contrasts and repetitions of texture, form and colour.

STREWN FLOWERS

The origins of the custom of strewing (sometimes 'strowing' or 'strawing') flowers and herbs are lost in the past. The Ancient Romans are known to have strewn roses on banqueting tables and beds (our phrase 'a bed of roses' comes from this custom) and all kinds of flowers were scattered in the streets for processions (*see* **GREEK AND ROMAN**). When Christ rode into Jerusalem on the ass, St Matthew's gospel records that, 'others cut down branches from the trees and strawed them in the way'. In Britain in Tudor times floors were strewn with rushes, herbs and sweet-smelling flowers, even in the royal apartments. Queen Elizabeth I had a special 'strewing maid'. Petals on banqueting tables were known in the seventeenth century.

The custom continues today in various forms. The streets of Warsaw were spread with flowers when Pope John Paul II visited in 1983; flowers are tossed on to the ice at skating championships, and on theatre stages by first and last night audiences. The modern custom of throwing paper confetti or rose petals at weddings, and computer punchings and ticker-tape on important processions is a less happy development of strewn flowers.

STRIPPING WOOD

Tree ivy (*Hedera helix*), in particular, can easily be stripped of its bark. Soak the piece in water (bath or garden water tank if large) for several days to soften the outer bark, then start cutting and peeling that away with a fairly sharp pen-knife or old kitchen knife – not too sharp or it is easy to cut through slender branches. If the piece is very intricate it will be quite a long job, but well worth it. Return the ivy to soak whenever the task has to be left. For very difficult sharp angles pull rough sisal string to and fro, to rub away the bark. With ivy it is easy to recognize when you are down to the heartwood; the rest will come cleanly away.

Bleaching afterwards is a matter of personal preference, but ivy dries naturally to a pale biscuit colour if it is cut living from the tree. Older pieces may be darker and they can be bleached in about 1:10 solution, or stronger, of household bleach. Rinse, then allow the wood to dry out slowly.

SWAG

Dictionary definitions suggest two essentially different types of swags: the festoon of flowers, foliage and fruit fastened up at both ends and hanging in a curve; or a suspended cluster.

In other words, a swag can be a horizontal or vertical hanging assemblage of plant material. Just where either ceases to be a swag and becomes an elongated form or garland is not clear!

For competition work in Britain a swag is simply defined as 'an exhibit designed to hang'. Although a swag may be, and usually is, made on a backing of wood, hardboard, pegboard, polystyrene, etc., this does not show and simply acts as a base to work on. When using fresh flowers and foliage, soaked floral foam is wrapped in thin polythene and secured to the backing with a covering of wire mesh hooked firmly over half a dozen or so nails in the backboard (*see* **MECHANICS**).

Dried and preserved (or artificial) materials can be glued directly onto the backing to cover it and form the background of the design. If sufficient depth cannot be achieved with successive layers, then raised sections can be made by gluing on a piece of dry-foam, or adding a mound of slow-drying cement or household detergent powder mixed with a very little water to make a thick paste. Stems and leaves can be set into this but it dries fairly quickly so have everything needed ready to complete the design quickly. Ribbons, cords, shells, small cherubs, etc. can be incorporated as necessary.

SWIRLY TREES

Swirly or 'whirly' trees, zigzags, or spirals, call them what you will, are pretty and elegant decorations where height is needed and space is limited, e.g., at the chancel steps in church for a wedding or on either side of a door or archway.

The mechanics are shown on page 117 and a drawing on page 180. It is important that the stand is heavy enough, at the base, to be stable. The effect of a 'double Hogarth' as it was once called, can only be achieved successfully with curving sprays of foliage or blossom. If the arrangement stands with its back to a wall, then it is very economical of flowers. An attractive all-round effect can be achieved if the ledges for the containers are fixed *round* the centre stake facing in different directions, but this will take much more plant material, of course, as the back of the arrangement on each ledge needs to be carefully filled in.

SYMBOLISM

Floral symbolism goes back to antiquity and has taken many forms over the centuries. The lotus, the blue water-lily of the River Nile, symbolized Isis, the goddess of the Ancient Egyptians. The rose has represented not only the Virgin Mary but also, in earlier mythology, Venus, goddess of love. Today it is the emblem of England.

Religious symbolism is referred to in both the **Renaissance** and the **Dutch/Flemish** entries. Renaissance artists included the Madonna lily as the symbol of the Virgin in many paintings, also the pink ('divine love' if in the Virgin's hand) and the crown imperial (for Christ, the King of Heaven). Violets signified humility, and aquilegia the seven gifts of the Holy Ghost.

In the 'vanitas' paintings of the Netherlands in the seventeenth and eighteenth centuries, broken stems and marred and cut fruits symbolized decay and were a reminder of the Calvinist doctrine of the futility and brevity of man's own life.

Doctrine of Signatures

At least until the eighteenth century (and in country districts till well into the nineteenth) physicians and herbalists believed in the 'Doctrine of Signatures'. Medicines then were made from plants and herbs, or 'simples' as they were called, and the colour, texture or shape of the plant was believed to indicate which part of the body or what illness it might cure. For example, jaundice might be cured by the yellow bark of berberis, or turmeric or the yellow juice of the celandine; brain troubles by the walnut because both were convoluted in form; plants with stems speckled like a snake were used to cure snakebite and stings; and the bright blue speedwell with its black and white centre was called 'eyebright' and used to heal sore eyes.

Romantic symbolism

It was the Victorians, in the nineteenth century, who brought flower symbolism to its romantic peak with their 'Language of Flowers'.

Its origins lie mistily in antiquity. It is thought that the Ancient Greeks had a system of messages by flowers, as did the Chinese, Turks and Persians. From them versions were introduced into France and Germany (*Blumen-Sprache*) and were known in Britain at least as early as the beginning of the eighteenth century. It was essentially a language for lovers, though meanings attributed to flowers still retained many of their religious and medical connotations. The Victorians (in the age of chaperones for young ladies) developed the language so that scarcely a plant was overlooked, and by mid-century code-books were being published rather like dictionaries: you could either look up the flower for its meaning, or look up what messages you wished to convey and find the flower or plant which conveyed it. (Surely chaperones could do this, too?) Meanings did not always accord from one book to another and complications arose when the *way* in which the flower was used changed the meaning.

Floral symbolism continues, though less frenetically, to this day. Poppies are still a symbol for the dead of World War I, red roses are sent by lovers on St Valentine's Day, shamrocks are worn on St Patrick's Day and white heather is for luck.

TABLE DECORATIONS

Floral decorations on meal tables were not general until the middle of the nineteenth century when they developed into elaborate displays, especially at banquets and high-society dinners.

Table decorations as classes at Royal Horticultural Society shows began in 1861 and continued in great popularity at all types of flower shows until the 1970s, when interest began to slacken and table classes at shows have dwindled since then. The reasons may be conjectured: space is needed to stage full scale tables; the cost to exhibitors is prohibitive as cloths often have to be supplied as well as flowers; the tableware, candlesticks, etc. are vulnerable to theft; and today the family dinner table is rarely set in a formal manner.

Table decorations fall, generally, into two categories: for a seated meal and for a buffet. Some general considerations apply to both:

1 **Colour** should be related to china, table linen, the occasion (e.g., golden wedding), or food (e.g., Chinese, Mexican, seafood). As the table should be 'the cynosure of all eyes', as Constance Spry puts it, links with the general room decor will be less important, though it may give a lead. Colour is

Table Decoration *Clipped leaves, tulips and driftwood suit the modern chunky pottery and rush mats on a pine table.*

especially important in the evening when a meal will be taken in artificial light, perhaps just by candlelight. All dark colours, blues and purples will look black, and it is safest to use paler tints, yellows and white which show up well.

2 **Plant material** should be clean and well-groomed as it is near food and will be seen at close quarters.

3 **Mechanics** must be secure and well hidden, because the arrangement may get knocked and will be seen close to.

4 **Scents:** strong scents should be avoided; they may conflict with the food and be unacceptable to some guests.

5 **Style:** the degree of formality of the meal governs the laying of the table and the choice of china, linen, glass and cutlery (flatware). The table flowers should reflect this and be in keeping. The branched silver candelabra, for example, with orchids and carnations, will be out of place with rush placemats and hand-thrown pottery.

Seated meal

The size of the table and number of guests/family will determine how much space can be allowed for the flowers, but much depends on whether the meal will be served from a sideboard or hostess trolly, or from the table itself. The height of the flower arrangement should never interfere with conversation across the table, except at grand banquets perhaps. Generally, it should be under 30 cm (12 in.), which accounts for the enduring popularity of the long low table arrangement. Raised slightly on a base or in a footed container, the flowers and leaves are kept out of the way of dishes. If the decoration is to be two-tiered, there should be sufficient space between the top and bottom tiers to allow cross-table conversation.

Buffet tables

The accent here is on greater height and impact, but the decoration must be stable as people will be moving about, serving themselves and jostling the table. The placement of the arrangement will depend on whether guests will be moving round on all sides or whether one (usually long) side of the table will be against a wall. Remember that people are standing in front of a buffet table so consider whether it is worth while expending a lot of effort on garlanding and swagging the cloth when it will be seen only by the first few who come to be served.

Candles

Candles, whether in low holders or tall sticks, provide welcome verticals in table settings which tend to be rather flat. (*See* **CANDLES**)

Table decorations at shows

Whereas American show schedules are specific about the type of table setting to be staged and for what number, schedules in Britain judged under NAFAS rules, usually state only if it is to be a buffet or seated meal. Neither need be for functional use. Sometimes the space allocated is only about 60 cm (2 ft) square and here it is intended that this area should represent the table centre. All tables are judged from a standing position and (except for buffets) from a seated position as well.

Check whether it is permitted to decorate the corners and sides of tables, outside the stated table measurements.

TAPES

Clear, general purpose	Sellotape, Holdfast, 3 M Scotch available in widths 12–25 mm ($\frac{1}{2}$–1 in.).
Clear invisible	Does not discolour with age or show when photocopied, e.g., Scotch 'Magic'.
Clear double-sided	Tough vinyl tape coated both sides with removable backing paper. Virtually invisible.
Plastic	Waterproof PVC, several colours, 19 mm ($\frac{3}{4}$ in.) wide.
Drafting	High-tack paper tape for sealing picture frames, etc.
Masking	Low-tack paper tape, for fixing stems when pressing, cropping photos. 19–50 mm ($\frac{3}{4}$–2 in.) wide.
Stem-binding	Formerly gutta-percha, now thin plastic (e.g., Guttaroll) or waxed paper. It stretches slightly and adheres to itself with the warmth of the hand. 12 mm ($\frac{1}{2}$ in.) wide in green, brown, white.
Oasis tape	Sludge-green waterproof tape, 5 and 12 mm wide ($\frac{1}{4}$–$\frac{1}{2}$ in.), for securing floral foam or wire-netting into containers.
Oasis fix	Green, strong-hold putty adhesive, 12 mm ($\frac{1}{2}$ in.) wide in rolls on removable paper backing.

TEACHER

A flower arrangement teacher may (a) be fully qualified as a teacher and taking part-time classes in the subject, or (b) have taken part-time training for teaching in adult education and hold a City and Guilds or local education authority certificate. In flower clubs teachers of beginners groups may simply be experienced club members. Because of this wide range of teaching (as opposed to flower arranging) ability and experience, the **NAFAS Teachers' Association** (q.v.) was formed to help the exchange of ideas and knowledge.

TEXTURE

Texture is one of the **design elements** (q.v.). It refers to the surface quality and character of any object, man-made or natural. It may be visual or tactile. The flower arranger is mainly concerned with *visual* texture as arrangements are seen rather than handled – except in the process of arranging.

Plant material offers textures of every kind:

velvety – rose petal
glossy – camellia leaf
prickly – teasel stem
ridged – hogweed stem
satiny – tulip petal
nobbly – warty gourd
rough – driftwood
felty – stachys leaves (lamb's ears)

These characteristics can be used effectively in **interpretative** arranging (q.v.), where the value of texture in helping to 'tell the story' should never be overlooked.

Containers, bases, accessories and backgrounds offer a similar range and an effective design will have sufficient variations of texture to give interest, with some repetitions and some contrasts. If an arrangement lacks 'life' it is often because there is not enough variation in the surfaces.

Texture is important in all types of flower arrangements, but especially so in:

- dried and preserved arrangements which are often monochrome, in tints and shades of brown. Different textures play their part in adding interest.
- foliage or green arrangements. In spite of the huge range of greens, and the varied shapes and sizes of leaves, a foliage arrangement needs changes of texture. If all the surfaces are shiny, for example, the effect is uninteresting; if they are all matt, something is needed to enliven them.
- in modern **free-style** (q.v.) and **abstract** (q.v.) designs. Modern painting, sculpture, furniture and architecture rely on the use of texture to provide interest and decoration. In flower arrangements in these styles, which do not rely on conventional prettiness for impact, the textures of the plant material chosen are of paramount importance.
- in **still life** (q.v.) designs, especially those using fruit and/or vegetables. Painters liked to show their skill in portraying different textures; the arranger has to achieve an interesting grouping of the real thing.

Visual texture is affected by light and the angle from which it falls. Think of the concertina-like formation of a palm leaf: with light shining directly on it the look is of lines radiating like a fan on a more or less flat surface; take the light to one side and the effect is of sharp regular ridges. Low, side lighting creates shadows which enhance textural qualities.

Texture affects colour. Identical red hues will look brighter on a smooth glossy surface and darker on a matt rough one. This characteristic can be used to create colour variations in an arrangement.

THORN STRIPPERS

A very simple but handy tool (*see* **TOOLS AND EQUIPMENT** page 167) which, if pulled sharply down a stem, will strip it of thorns, spines, prickles and leaves in one movement. It is invaluable for preparing stems of roses, teasels, solidago, Michaelmas daisies, etc.

TIED BUNCH, *see* HAND BUNCH

TITLES ON EXHIBITS

Show schedules frequently require 'the title to be stated' in interpretative classes where a wide choice of subject is possible, such as 'Book at bed-time', 'A night at the opera', 'Headline news' or 'A page from hstory'.

This displayed title is considered to be part of the exhibit, so it should be well thought out, well executed and well placed. A typed or handwritten rectangle of white card is rarely appropriate and is very eye-catching, likely to unbalance the whole exhibit visually.

Try always to link the title with the style and theme of the whole exhibit, e.g., written on a dried or glycerined leaf for 'Autumn foliage'; in period lettering for a period piece; on a flat pebble for a seascape or wood for a landscape; or as a tiny open book (but tint the pages to beige) for a literary theme. (*See* LETTERING)

TOOLS AND EQUIPMENT

All that is absolutely necessary for flower arrangement is something to cut with and something to put the flowers in. Many people are content with that. But as in any other craft, the right tools and equipment make the task easier and more efficient, and, sometimes, more effective. Acquire 'the basics' as soon as possible; the rest can be added as and when needed. Each item is dealt with in more detail under its alphabetical entry; stem supports also come under MECHANICS.

Cutters

flower cutters | flower scissors | household scissors | knife | wire cutters | garden sécateurs | thorn strippers

wire & string

2″ (5 cm) mesh | 1″ (2 cm) mesh | reel wire | stub wire | silver or rose wire | coat hanger | green garden twine

for water

buckets | household with swing handle | misting spray | tall with side handles | long-spout can

sticks | wooden kebab sticks | cocktail sticks

tapes & strip adhesives

oasis tape | sellotape single & double sided | oasis-fix

stem binding tape in green brown & white | plasticine

Basics
buckets
containers
cutters or scissors
floral foam
foam anchor(s) – plastic or metal
knife
Oasis-fix, sealing strip or Plasticine
pinholder 8 cm (3 in.)
spray – for misting
tape – Oasis tape or alternative
watering can, long spout
wire netting – 1 cm ($\frac{1}{2}$ in.) and 5 cm (2 in.)

Additions
candle cup(s)
cocktail sticks/tooth picks
cones – plastic
driftwood – screw/clamp
plastic sheeting
pliers – fine-nosed
saw – small folding
secateurs – garden type
skewers – wooden kebab
stembind tape
thorn strippers
twine – green garden
wire cutters
wires –reel, rose and stubs

A toolbox, bag or basket is useful for keeping working tools in one place and at hand whenever needed. The cantilevered workman's toolbox is useful, or many arrangers use the plastic household baskets intended for cleaning materials and dusters.

TOPPING UP

It is estimated that cut plant material will take up 75 per cent of the water it will need for the next two or three days, in the first 10–12 hours. So the water level in a container will need topping up, perhaps twice in the first day and once a day thereafter. Mist-spraying when possible reduces the water loss through transpiration. Floral foams dry out quickly, at the top first, so stems pushed in only a little way can soon be starved of water. Using a long-spouted can (or a teapot in an emergency), dribble a little water onto the foam first. Leave it to soak in, then complete topping up the container to within 1 cm ($\frac{1}{2}$ in.) of the rim. Check that no drips are marking polished wood, or fabric, and that no water is 'syphoning' out down a leaf.

TRADITIONAL

Traditional will mean different things in different countries with different cultures. In western-style flower arrangements, at least, it is taken to mean a formal massed design, not necessarily triangular in outline; it may be oval or fan-shaped or curving, but will have little space within the design.

TRANSITION

Transition in flower arrangement describes a graded sequence between large and small, dark and light, pointed and round, thick and thin, etc. It provides the gradual link from one extreme to the other: e.g., orange is the transitional colour between red and yellow, being composed from the two primary colours. Opening buds, then partly open flowers provide the transition between a tight bud and a full-blown rose. Gentle transition is a feature of traditional western massed arranging, but is little used in freestyle and abstract designs where sharper contrasts make for impact.

Transition in size, shape, colour or line is one of the ways of achieving **rhythm** (q.v.) within any design.

TRAY CLASSES

Occasionally seen in Britain, but more popular in America, are show classes for a laid tray with a suitable flower decoration. The occasion (breakfast, TV supper, invalid meal, etc.) should be stated in the schedule. To be practical, since the tray will be carried, the floral decoration cannot be large and a problem arises under NAFAS rules which require plant material to predominate. Perhaps this explains their lack of popularity here – it's a pity. Trays make an attractive open-staging class for shows, with interesting colour combinations and pretty or strikingly patterned china and linen. The viewing public enjoys finding ideas to use at home.

TREES

Decorative or 'topiary' trees, popular with arrangers, can be made in many ways, shapes and sizes from 15 cm (6 in.) tinies to large-scale 2 m (6 ft) features.

It is essential, whatever the size, to have an absolutely vertical 'trunk' set in plaster of Paris, Polyfilla or cement, in a plastic flower pot or tin which is large enough to make the tree absolutely stable. This can be painted or decorated with fabric and braid or put inside a decorative basket, urn or

Trees *Decorative trees take many forms.*

cachepot. The trunk may be of dowelling or a broom handle or more interestingly, because of its colour and texture, of natural wood with bark. Take great care to see that it is vertical from every angle before the plaster or cement finally sets. Use a spirit level to be sure. If the trunk has a twist, it must *look* vertical.

The mechanics for the top can be a ball of moss in 2 cm ($\frac{3}{4}$ in.) plastic or wire netting or a roughly circular block of floral foam, again in netting for additional strength. If fresh plant materials are to be used it is sensible to wrap the soaked foam in thin drycleaners' polythene *before* the netting. Impale this ball onto the trunk. If there is any danger of it slipping down, put a nail at right-angles through the trunk at the bottom of the ball. (For a small tree just crumple several layers of clear adhesive tape round the trunk at this point.) If a cone is being used to make a pyramidal tree, work in same way.

Plant materials

Evergreens are the most popular material for covering the tree. Short pieces of the bushy types are the most useful, like box and cupressus, and holly at Christmas. Once the tree is covered it can be sheared all over like a clipped topiary tree in the garden, or left as it is. Flowers, fruit, berries or cones can then be added. Cones will need to be given wire stems, and fruit can be impaled with cocktail or kebab sticks. But there are many other variations on this theme: dried and preserved leaves can be used, or dried flowers like helichrysums (straw-flowers); in the height of summer, fresh flowers look pretty and wedding-like; fruits and vegetables on a moss basis are interesting for a party; ribbon loops and bows can be interspersed on any festive tree; and baubles can be added at Christmas time. Artificial flowers or fruits can be mixed with fresh or preserved foliages, which is less expensive than using all artificial materials.

Another kind of tree, with naturalistic branches, can be made from plastic fern and leaf sprays (widely available at Christmas). Each large spray can be broken down into small pieces and then wired and taped to make 'branches' which, in turn, are assembled into a 'trunk'. This is set in a rough lump of plaster of Paris or Polyfilla on a base and hung with tiny baubles, wired beads, plastic fruits, or sequins.

Recently popular have been trees of reindeer moss on foam or a wire-mesh shape packed with moss or broken pieces of foam. Soak the dried moss first to remove the bits of stick and debris, then use it while still damp as it is much easier to handle. Make U-shaped hairpins from stub wires to secure the moss to the framework.

Ribbon bows and streamers tied round the trunk give a festive look. If the tree is to be out of doors, be sure the ribbon is waterproof.

(For diagrams *see* **MECHANICS**; *see also* **SWIRLY TREES**)

TRIMMING LEAVES

It is often possible to trim round the outside of leaves if they are *either* too large for your purpose *or* marked or eaten at the edges. Most tough, evergreen leaves will stand this treatment, for example: aucuba, bergenia, laurel, mahonia and privet. Thinner textured leaves, such as most hostas, tend to go brown at the cut after a while.

For the neatest finish use household scissors rather than flower cutters. It is permissible to trim leaves in this way at competitive shows, but needs to be carefully done if the judge is not to downpoint for poor finish.

TUDOR (1485–1600)

The Tudor period offers the first real evidence in Britain of flower arrangements indoors. During the sixteenth century Renaissance ideas were being developed in a period of comparative peace following the Wars of the Roses. Trade with Mediterranean countries and the East made Britain a strong maritime power like Holland, with a powerful and wealthy merchant middle class. Pleasure gardens were possible for the first time as new manor houses, rather than castles, were being built. They featured enclosed knot gardens and clipped topiary trees and hedges.

Exploration and discovery – geographical, scientific, botanic, literary and artistic – were the hallmarks of the century.

Settings

Timbered buildings with exposed beams outside and in; oak and elm wood, carved, and as linenfold panelling; plastered walls brightly decorated or hung with painted cloths or tapestries; rush and herb-strewn floors; casement windows with small panes of glass, square or diamond-shaped; floral motifs in tapestries and embroideries for furnishings and clothes; rush-nip lights; simple pewter utensils and treen; velvet and brocade fabrics for the rich, fustian (dark twill) and russet (coarse homespun) for the poor.

Colours

Bright primary colours on walls and ceilings; embroidery silks and imported fabrics in jewel colours; external plasterwork painted orange, yellow and pink.

Plant material

The gillyflower ('July-flower'), which seems to have included pinks, carnations, wallflowers, sweet williams and stocks, is typical of the sixteenth

tussie-mussie held in the hand

foxglove from 16ᵗʰ ms.

rush-nip light & pewter table-ware

from a Holbein painting c.1527

Tudor *Tudor (1485–1600) flowers and settings.*

century. The herb rosemary was also commonly used at weddings and funerals and for strewing on floors because of its pungent smell. Many other herbs such as thyme, marjoram, rue, lavender and sage were popular, as were fragrant flowers such as honeysuckle, monarda, primrose, woodruff, daffodil, rose and lily. Iris, aquilegia, pansy, cowslip and narcissus were also brought indoors with ivy, holly, yew, myrtle and juniper foliage. The herbalists, John Gerard and John Parkinson, and other writers, give us this information (*see also* **SHAKESPEARE'S FLOWERS**).

Containers
Pewter jugs and vases; simple decanter shapes in clear glass; treen (wooden bowls and cups).

Arrangements and uses
1 Dried petals and herbs were used for **pot pourri** (q.v.) and **pomanders** (q.v.) were carried.
2 Tussie-mussies, or nosegays, were simple hand bunches of sweet-smelling herbs and flowers carried to ward off disease and to compensate for bad smells in sewer-like streets.
3 Holbein, the painter, shows us flowers used indoors in tall metal vases in Sir Thomas More's home; and in a simple glass vase on the desk of George Gisze, a merchant. The More painting shows iris, lilies, pinks, aquilegias, and possibly peonies, arranged with foliage clustered round the vase rim. The Gisze portrait shows three pinks or carnations, a sprig of rosemary and a tiny flower which could be woodruff.
4 **Garlands** (q.v.) were still used and worn as 'crown garlands' by priests at special church festivals, May queens and brides.
5 Be-ribboned 'bride cups' of flowers, wheat, rosemary or broom (these three often gilded) were carried before the bride at weddings.
6 Floors were strewn with rushes, herbs and flowers (even in Queen Elizabeth's private apartments). (*See* **PERIOD ARRANGING**)

TWENTIETH-CENTURY STYLES
In almost anything you can name, the twentieth century has seen more advances, discoveries and developments than the four centuries that preceded it. Flower arrangement is no exception.
    Three major factors have contributed to this:
1 the rapid rise of flower arrangement as an amateur hobby after the Second World War and the formation of flower clubs;
2 the introduction of **interpretation** (q.v.) in shows and exhibition work, which is unique to this century, and the latter part of it, in fact. This was the final factor which confirmed flower arrangement as an art form (however minor) with arrangers as artists and designers who had stories to tell, moods to convey and even social statements to make;
3 the development of modern **free-style** (q.v.) and **abstract** (q.v.) arrangements in the west, influenced by the spread of ikebana and the effect of modern trends in painting, sculpture, architecture and interior design.
The illustration opposite shows, in essence, the characteristics of flower arrangement in Britain, decade by decade, this century. Of course, many other styles developed in each decade, especially in the 1950s and 1960s when talks, articles and books, by Julia Clements and Violet Stevenson among others, spread ideas to the growing army of arrangers avid for knowledge.

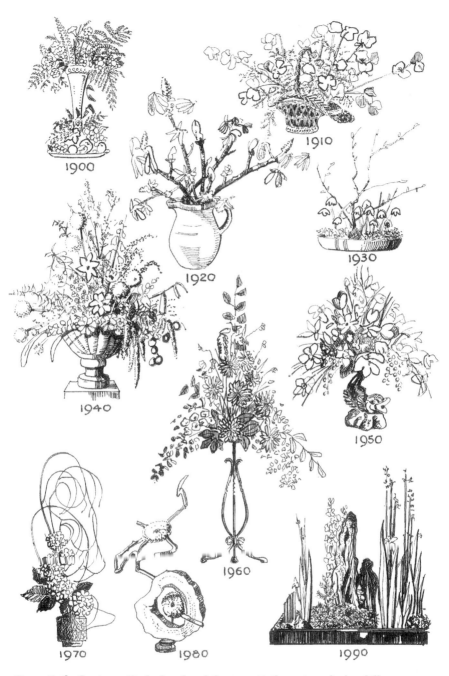

Twentieth Century *Each decade of the twentieth century had a different style which became popular. Will the 1990s produce something we have not yet seen?*

1900   The tightly packed **Victorian** (q.v.) style in a trumpet-shaped vase and stand.

1910   Sweet peas and gypsophila typify the softer, more elegant style of the **Edwardians** (q.v.).

1920   Simple country styles.

1930   Still naturalistic, and the landscape design makes an appearance.

1940   The influence of Constance Spry shows in the groupings of mixed garden flowers in an urn. They are massed, but not tightly packed.

1950   The popular dolphin container with a fairly geometric triangular arrangement of mixed flowers and foliage.

1960   The English pedestal with a framework of foliage, highlighted with flowers.

1970   Line and space have become important. At first, the Americans and later Marian Aaronson in Britain explored new ground.

1980   Design and non-naturalism are the key to **abstract** (q.v.) arranging.

1990   The continental grouping in verticals, horizontals and blocks of colour. Will this be the style of the 90s?

(*See* **ART DECO**, **ART NOUVEAU** *and* **NINETEEN TWENTIES AND THIRTIES**)

URN

Dictionaries define an urn as 'a vase with a foot and usually with a rounded body'. It is, perhaps, the favourite of all containers for the western flower arranger. The style of the Greek urn of antiquity has been handed down the centuries in the west and has featured in most ages from the sturdy terracotta urns familiar in Dutch/Flemish paintings to the gilded and elegantly classical ones of France in the rococo and directoire periods. English eighteenth-century porcelain was also produced in many urn shapes.

Today these styles are cheaply available in plastic, in all sizes and shapes and can be decorated, painted or sprayed in any colour or finish. For large displays, in church or stately home, garden urns are adaptable and can be on raised plinths for greater height and importance. Light in weight (a great advantage in moving and transporting), these urns sometimes need sand or shingle at the bottom to give them stability.

Classical

Dutch/Flemish

French rococo

C18 porcelain

VEGETABLES, *see* **FRUIT**

VICTORIAN 1830–1900

The Industrial Revolution in Britain and the development of railways and canals, changed the life of many from rural to urban. It also brought about the wealth of the middle-class factory and mill-owners and shopkeepers, and emphasized the great poverty of the working classes which gave rise to socialism later in the century. The class structure was rigid, and social conventions sacrosanct. Patriotism ran high, with pride in the British Empire and respect for the Queen in her widowhood. Except in the poorer classes, women did not go out to work and young ladies were expected to occupy themselves with duties in the home, education, handicrafts and charity work.

Settings
Victorian Gothic buildings, often red-brick with gables, turrets, dormers, porches and slate roofs; cast-iron railings, gates, garden furniture; overstuffed furniture padded with horsehair; deep-buttoned upholstery; blinds, net/lace curtains and velvet, chenille or damask drapes with fringes and bobbles; large overmantels to marble or cast-iron fireplaces; mahogany, rosewood and walnut furniture; conservatories. Gardens had formal bedding schemes, shrubberies and ferneries and towards the end of the period Gertrude Jekyll's and William Robinson's herbaceous borders and 'wild gardens' were popular.

Colours
The mid-century invention of aniline dyes brought rather harsh colours in violet, puce, deep red, grassy green, mustard yellow and light navy blue. Colour combinations were often garish, with contrasts preferred to toning schemes. Yellow was recommended in flower arrangements as an accent to make the other colours vivid.

Plant material
Ferns of every kind, smilax and ivies head the list of foliages used for indoor decoration, with flowers that were striped, streaked, blotched, speckled or of unusual shapes such as fuchsia, antirrhinum and calceolaria, and bell-shapes (lily-of-the-valley, bluebell, campanula, lily). Anything we think of today as an 'old-fashioned' flower was much used – phlox, pink, sweet william, rose, pansy, geranium, etc. Plant hunters had brought most of the shrubs and flowers we have today to British gardens, and hybridists were already increasing the size and range of colours. Indoor plants, though more limited in range, enjoyed a vogue comparable to today's interest in house plants. The aspidistra, parlour palm, mignonette and ferns were in every home. The pineapple was still a status symbol, as were other greenhouse fruits such as melons, peaches, grapes and nectarines.

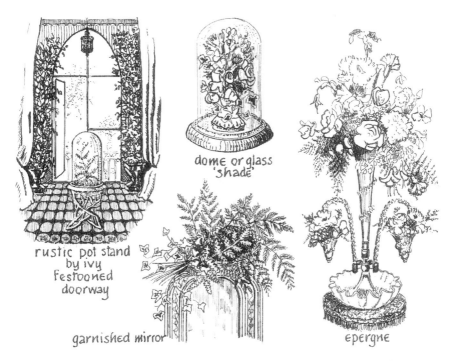

rustic pot stand
by ivy
festooned
doorway

dome or glass
'shade'

garnished mirror

epergne

Victorian *The clutter of Victoriana (1840–1900).*

Containers

The variety of shapes was endless, in glass, ceramics, metal and basketware. Vases were usually trumpet-shaped or with very narrow necks, often footed or decorated with appliqué flowers, leaves and rustic work. The epergne (a centre ornament for the dinner table, usually of glass) and the March stand were popular, as were shells, baskets, small posyholders, hand-vases and wall cornucopias.

Containers stood on a doily of crochet or lace-edged fabric, or a hand-embroidered mat, sometimes even of moss glued to a cardboard circle.

Arrangements and uses

The style of arranging was tightly massed and arrangements were called 'bouquets' even when in water.

1 Most typical of the later Victorian era is the table centrepiece either in an epergne or March stand, flanked with other trumpet vases of flowers and trails of leaves or fern between the place settings. Smilax may festoon the sides of the damask cloth with posies at the table corners or between place settings.

2 Small arrangements in bowls and vases were dotted about a living-room – possibly six to eight, either of one type of flower or a mixture of flowers, 'greens' (foliage) and grasses.

3 Indoor plants, especially ivy, were trained to frame and festoon mirrors, windows, doorways, even the banisters.

4 Tall vases or jars of dried flowers and leaves made permanent winter decorations; grasses (including pampas), palms, cereals, artichokes, everlastings, ferns, seedheads and pressed leaves or sprays were used.

Smaller dried arrangements, and 'phantoms' (from skeletonized leaves and seedheads) were protected under glass domes.

5 Church decorations were popular in the last half of the century. For religious festivals fresh flowers and greens were used for the altar, font, pulpit, windows and pillars, as today. 'Devices' were made of cardboard, zinc or wire-netting shapes to display texts, and patterns of flowers and leaves were either glued on or pushed through the holes.

6 Personal flowers were worn by ladies at all times of the day – at the neck, shoulder, bosom, waist, in the hair, on a muff or bonnet, or edging the hem of an evening dress. Posies were carried in the day and evening.

7 Artificial flowers were made in shells, wool, wax, leather, seaweed, feathers, fish-bones, silver paper, butterfly wings, tinsel, ribbon, paper and even hair.

Symbolism
'The Language of Flowers' reached the height of its popularity and was used for messages of love and sympathy (see SYMBOLISM).
(See PERIOD ARRANGING)

VIDEOS AND FILMS
In spite of the massive increase in films and videos in recent years, there are still very few dealing with flower arrangement. Jean Taylor made several short instruction films in the mid-1970s, and these are now available as videos. They deal with drying and preserving, and mechanics for small and large scale arrangements, and are available from Gerard Holdsworth Productions.

Bill Lomas made two one-hour long videos in 1985, dealing with 'The Basics' and 'A Step Further' on video cassettes in the 'Master Class' series. All are available in VHS or BETAMAX. (See APPENDIX: ADDRESSES)

VIRGIN MARY, PLANTS OF, see BIBLE PLANTS

WAFA

The World Association of Flower Arrangers was formed in London in 1981 to bring together the flower arranging organizations of countries all over the world, regardless of race, creed or colour. The official languages are English and French. The administration is by one member country/organization for three years, when it passes to another member. Great Britain organized WAFA for the first three years, 1981–4, followed by Belgium 1984–7, France 1987–90, Canada 1990–3 and New Zealand 1993–6. During each three year session, an international residential course, a general assembly and a world show are held.

Member countries pay a per capita subscription to WAFA, and each member of an affiliated club or society in those member countries is *ipso facto* a member of WAFA.

WATER-RETAINING MATERIAL

Many show rules (including NAFAS) require that fresh plant materials (other than fruit, vegetables, cacti, succulents, lichen and moss) should be staged in water or water-retaining material so that everything is maintained in good condition throughout the show. Water retaining materials are usually considered to include soaked floral foams, the age-old stand-bys moss and sand, also fruit, vegetables, earth and peat.

It is important, of course, that the moss, sand, earth and peat are soaked with water to provide enough moisture.

WEDDINGS

Flower arrangers are often asked by family or friends to do the wedding flowers. Be sure that you understand what you are to undertake, what money is available (a prepared estimate is sensible) and who will pay and when. A full-scale wedding can be a sizeable project which has to be carried out within a limited time, and you may need helpers. Whether or not a fee is charged will depend on many things: some groups do wedding flowers for their church flower fund or a church charity; some flower club members do so for other charities, etc. It is essential that this should be agreed at the outset, because few 'non-arrangers' have any idea of the amount of work involved and the cost of buying flowers. Colour(s) too must be agreed and the style to be aimed at, e.g., simple country wedding, period piece or town sophistication.

Personal flowers

These may be worn or carried by the bride, bridesmaids, principal and other guests and may take the form of head-dresses, bouquets, posies, baskets,

1: pew ends
2: pedestal at chancel steps
3: low flowers on altar   4: swirly trees   5: garlanded
pulpit   6: tiered flowers for a buffet table   7: hanging ball
8: posies & fabric swaging   9: topiary trees
10: garland & cake top-knot   11: swag on marquee pole
12: small table flowers

Weddings *Possible wedding decorations for church and reception.*

flower balls, corsages and buttonholes. These are all tasks for a competent
florist and unless you are, don't tackle them. *Consult:* bride and mother and
perhaps the local florist for them.

Church, chapel, etc.
The amount of money available will usually decide how much decoration is
possible in the church, though a good deal can be done very cheaply with

foliage and old man's beard (*Clematis vitalba*), Queen Anne's lace (*Anthriscus sylvestris*), catkins, etc. in season. The size of the church and the number of expected guests are important factors too. Remember that in Lent flowers may have to be minimal or they may not be allowed at all. If money is limited flowers are usually restricted to the chancel steps where most of the ceremony takes place and perhaps at the altar and the entrance porch or door. Pew ends (*see* **CHURCH FLOWERS**) are good value for time and money spent and bring flowers into the body of the church near the guests. A small arrangement in the vestry is a welcome touch for the register signing.

If economy is not the main factor then consider more pedestals or columns at appropriate points; **swirly trees** (q.v.); baskets on literature tables or chests; window arrangements; garlands to pulpit, lectern and other features; topiary trees outside the porch and so on. It is usual to repeat the colours of the bridal flowers in the church decorations. *Consult:* the clergy; the flower rota organizer (an important lady who must not be overlooked) and the rota arrangers for the week; the church secretary or verger about keys and access; other brides if there is more than one wedding on that same day.

Reception
This may be held at an hotel or restaurant, the bride's own home or a hired hall. It may be indoors or in a marquee. Each requires a slightly different approach.

Hotel or restaurant: You will have to ask to be allowed to undertake the flowers. Access in advance may be a problem. Make sure table layout is known and where pedestals etc. may stand. *Consult:* the catering manager.

Bride's home: Often a marquee is erected in the garden or for a smaller wedding the lounge and dining room are used. There is not usually a lot of space for flowers. Consider keeping them up out of the way: hanging baskets, swags, garlands, wall sconces, flower balls. *Consult:* the bride and mother; caterers.

Marquee: Uneven ground is the worst problem and, possibly, shortage of time if the marquee is erected late. Marquees with poles enable flowers to be put high up and hanging balls/baskets are possible. *Consult:* marquee erectors (*re* time) and caterers.

Hall: Hired halls tend to be impersonal and the colour of decor and furnishings can be a real problem! Concentrate on the tables (buffet style or laid for sit-down meal), the place where the bride will receive the guests and a cake-table if there is room. *Consult:* caretaker of hall *re* keys and access, also any regulations; and the caterers.

Cake table
Whatever the venue, if space permits, a separate round table for the cake is an attractive feature. It provides a focal point for speeches and the cake-cutting, especially if there is no top table at a buffet reception. Take care with its cloth, skirting and decoration, and make sure it is understood whether you, or the caterers, or the cake-maker will provide flowers for the top.

In all these matters the bride and her mother may be happy to leave the floral decorations entirely in your hands but their wishes, when stated, must be scrupulously respected. You may have to make all the suggestions and be guided by their reactions.

It will probably be necessary for you to provide all the containers for the various venues and ensure the collection and return to their owners afterwards. Check early on if flowers or foliage may be cut from the bride's family's gardens and what is likely to be available. Place orders with florists and nurseries in good time and be prepared to have to make quick alterations if various flowers or colours are not available at the last minute.

Foliage
Try to keep this as light as possible, avoiding too many dark, solid-looking evergreens. Variegated leaves are invaluable, especially if flowers are not plentiful because of the season or cost. White and cream leaf variegation goes well with pink, blue or mauve flowers and lime-green or yellow variegations with yellow, apricot or rust flowers. White flowers mix well with either. Grey leaves provide another light-coloured foil, but use them with discretion; too much tends to make arrangements look shabby. To achieve a pretty, romantic effect ferns of all kinds, feathery cupressus, heathers, 'sugar' pine (Western hemlock) and small-leaved ivy trails are useful. Foliage can be picked, prepared and **conditioned** (q.v.) several days in advance of use and kept standing in a cool, shady place in deep water.

Flowers
Any flowers, even quite short-lived ones like sweet peas, can be used for weddings as they are only needed, as a rule, to last for the important day. Some white or cream flowers will almost certainly be needed to lighten any chosen colour scheme, be it pink, mauve, blue, yellow or apricot. If white only is wanted, then aim to get a variety and use creams as well – otherwise the effect can be surprisingly stark. Gypsophila, with its lacy small flowers, is available from florists all the year round nowadays. Whatever colour scheme is used, variations within its range, from palest to darkest, will add interest and depth to all arrangements. Too careful colour matching can produce a very dead-pan look. Blue, even in high summer, can look cold in a darkish church and needs white and tints of pinkish-mauve to warm it up.

Collect florist- and nursery-cut flowers at least two days in advance of arranging. They are usually not fully open and may be in tight bud, so they need a day or two, standing in deep water, and perhaps even in sun or the warmth of the house, to open to their peak for the important day.

WIRE CUTTERS
An essential tool in the arranger's work-box is something with which to cut wires and wire-netting. Special wire cutters are illustrated on page 167. You can also use the notch in flower scissors or the cutting slot in pliers. A word of warning: *don't* ruin your best secateurs by using them to cut wires.

WIRE NETTING
Wire netting is variously called wire mesh and chicken wire and is shown under **MECHANICS** and **TOOLS AND EQUIPMENT**.

British arrangers generally prefer the bare wire (not coated) and a fine gauge so that it is easy to handle and malleable. Plastic-coated wire is also available in many countries. Netting may be bought at hardware stores and garden centres, but you may have to search to find one willing to cut short lengths from a roll. A square metre or yard is sufficient for a beginner to start with for two or three containers. Cut off any selvedge before use. Use 5 cm (2 in.) mesh for crumpling in a container as a stem support and 2 cm (¾ in.) or 1 cm (⅜ in.) mesh for a cap to be wired over a piece of floral foam as an additional support in case the foam begins to break up.

When crumpled netting is used it should (1) provide four or five layers of holes to hold stems firmly; (2) be domed well above the container rim to take stems curving down and out sideways; and (3) be secured with wire, string or rubber bands criss-crossed over the mesh and round the container, or with Oasis tape (*see* **TAPES**) taken over the mesh and down the sides of the container where it will be hidden by the arrangement.

WIRES

Although flower arrangers are less concerned with wiring fresh flowers than is usual and acceptable in floristry, there are many ways in which the arranger finds wiring useful and even essential, especially with dried, preserved and artificial plant materials. These are some of the wires likely to be needed:

Stub wires
These are used as false stems for dried, preserved and artificial flowers and leaves: inserted into hollow stems, or spiralled round limp stems, to strengthen them. Stub wires are now available in metric sizes, which replace the old gauge numbers (swg = standard wire gauge).

Wire gauge measures (thickness)

General size	Thickness in mm (Swg No.)	
Heavy	1·25 (18) 1·00 (19) 0·90 (20)	The sizes most often needed are 0.90 mm (20 swg) for flowers like large chrysanthemums, 0.71 mm (22 swg) (the most popular) for roses, carnations, cones, etc., and 0.56 mm (24 swg) for small roses, pinks and general bouquet work.
Medium	0·71 (22) 0·56 (24)	
Fine	0·46 (26) 0·38 (28)	
Very fine	0·32 (30) 0·28 (32) 0·24 (34) 0·20 (36)	

Lengths range from 130 mm (5 in.) to 460 mm (18 in.)

Silver (rose) wires
0.38–0.28 mm (28–32 swg) are 180 mm (7 in.) long and used for fine work.

Silver reel wire
0.32–0.20 mm (26–36 swg) is used for bridal work, binding, making up artificial flowers, etc.

Apart from silvered and green and brown lacquered types, which are more expensive, florists' wires are usually 'blue-annealed', which helps them to bend easily, but does not make them rust-proof. Keep them as dry as possible. They are invariably taped with stem binding so that flowers are not marked.

Coat hanger wire

Give-away wire hangers from dry-cleaners, if pulled into a roughly circular shape, make an excellent basis for a round wreath at Christmas time.

WIRING

Wiring, to support and mount flowers and leaves, has always been associated with floristry rather than flower arranging. Since the advent of floral foams florists do much less wiring, especially for funeral work, but it is still the method of constructing bridal bouquets, corsages and head dresses.

Flower arrangers use wires to provide false stems for preserved and artificial flowers, leaves and seedheads; to mount **cones** (q.v.), ribbons and bows; to construct swags and garlands; and, occasionally, to strengthen a weak stem or to give extra support to a heavy flower head.

Wiring should be as invisible as possible. Use the finest gauge wire needed to do the job efficiently. Except for fine silver wires, all should be taped with stem-binding, either the present-day plastic substitute for gutta-percha or the waxy, crêpe paper strip which is easy to use and comparatively inexpensive. Both are available in white, brown and several shades of green. Most are 12 mm ($\frac{1}{2}$ in.) wide and for fine work with thin wires half or even one-third width makes for a much neater finish.

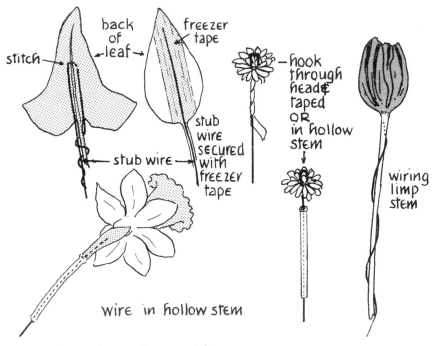

Wiring *Ways of wiring leaves and flower.*

The diagrams show methods of wiring leaves and flowers. Wiring is permissible at most competitive shows but should never be obtrusive; aim at as naturalistic a look as possible.

WORKSHOPS, *see* **DAY SCHOOLS**

WREATH

To many, a wreath has only funeral connotations, which is a great pity because the wreath, as a circular garland of leaves or flowers, has played a part in joyful celebrations since the days of Ancient Egypt and Greece. The circle stood for eternity, renewal and rebirth and became a triumphant symbol of victory over death.

The Ancient Greeks crowned the victors at their games with wreaths of olive, pine or laurel. In many countries marriage has been symbolized by a wreath of myrtle (Hebrew), hawthorn (Greek) and verbena (Roman); our own tradition of orange blossom for brides comes from the Saracens. The Romans awarded wreaths of oak leaves to one who saved life in battle (bravery) and to the Chinese a wreath of fragrant olives means literary merit. Christ's crown of thorns symbolized his triumphant martyrdom.

Today the custom continues in the welcoming *leis* of Hawaii and in the laurels hung round the necks of victorious racing drivers. The renewed popularity in Britain over the last decade or so of the Christmas door wreath – hung as a welcome and a greeting to all passers-by, visitors and guests – revives an ancient tradition.

A door wreath can be made on various foundations:
1 wire wreath frame.
2 wire coat hanger pulled into a circle.
   Both can be covered with overlapping small bunches of evergreens tied on with green twine and with wired fruit, cones or flowers twisted in.
3 floral foam in a circular plastic trough used for fresh materials. Short lengths soon obscure the plastic holder.
4 circular dry foam or polystyrene base used for artificial or dried and preserved foliage, seedheads and flowers. This is very light in weight and easy to hang on walls indoors.
5 Circular wreaths of straw, vines or pliable branches provide a base for decorations of all kinds.

In each case, ribbon bows and streamers, bells and baubles can be added as wished.

A wreath is also very effective as a table centre, on its own or round the base of candelabra, a group of low candle-holders or a Madonna at Christmas time. At weddings, in white or pastel flowers hung on walls or doors or laid on tables, wreaths symbolize the wedding ring.

XANTHIC

Xanthic means 'of or pertaining to yellow'. As the book needs an 'X' it is a good place to point out that Easter-time daffodils, primroses, celandines and forsythia, and golden wedding flowers are xanthic!

A Xanthic wreath for Spring using daffodils, primroses, berries of Ilex bacciflava and Ilex 'Golden King' leaves

YOUNG FLOWER ARRANGERS

Junior flower clubs and shows, popular for many years in America, are now finding greater interest in Britain. At the end of 1987 eleven junior clubs were affiliated to **NAFAS** (q.v.), all but one, curiously enough, in the north, North Wales and Scotland. Although youngsters are enthusiastic, it does require the continuing interest and encouragement of adults to keep a club going. NAFAS produces guidelines on club activities and a lesson syllabus.

Individual junior members are welcomed at a number of adult clubs, and children's classes for flower arrangement are a feature at many local and village shows.

The Duke of Edinburgh Award Scheme and *Girl Guides' badges* both encourage flower arrangement. The syllabuses are aimed at a good understanding of the craft, conservation and gardening.

Girl Guides'
flower arranger badge

ZODIAC

An A to Z book must have a 'z' to finish with, and the zodiac offers more scope than zinnia or zantedeschia, so here are the colours, stones, metals, and above all, the plants ascribed by the astrologers to the 12 signs of the zodiac.

Sign	Colour Metal Gemstone	Flowers	Trees Herbs and spices
Aries (Ram) 21 March– 20 April	Red Iron Diamond	Honeysuckle, thistle	Thorn-bearing trees Capers, mustard, cayenne pepper
Taurus (Bull) 21 April–21 May	Dark green or pink Copper Sapphire (sometimes emerald)	Rose, poppy, foxglove	Ash, cypress, apple, vines Cloves, sorrel, spearmint
Gemini *(The Twins)* 22 May–21 June	Most colours – yellow favourite Mercury Agate	Lily-of-the-valley	Nut-bearing trees Aniseed, marjoram, caraway
Cancer (Crab) 22 June–22 July	Silver grey Silver Pearl	Acanthus, convolvulus, white flowers in general	Trees rich in sap Verbena, tarragon
Leo (Lion) 23 July– 23 August	Colours of sun – sunrise to sunset Gold Ruby	Sunflower, marigolds	Palm, bay, laurel, orange and lemon Saffron, peppermint, rosemary
Virgo (Virgin) 24 August– 22 September	Navy blue, dark brown, green Mercury or nickel Sardonyx	All brightly coloured small flowers such as anemones	All nut-bearing trees (*see Gemini*) Herbs with bright yellow or blue flowers or colouring

Libra *(Scales/balance)* 23 September– 23 October	Blue – from pale to ultramarine, pinks, pale green Copper, sometimes bronze Sapphire, jade	Blue flowers, hydrangea, large roses	Ash, poplar Mint, arrack, cayenne
Scorpio (Scorpion) 24 October– 22 November	Dark red and maroon Steel, iron Opal	Geranium, rhododendron	Blackthorn and thick bushy trees Aloes, witch- hazel, catmint
Sagittarius *(Hunter/archer)* 23 November– 21 December	Dark or sky blue, purple Tin Topaz	Pinks and carnations	Lime, birch, mulberry, oak Sage, aniseed, balsam
Capricorn (Goat) 22 December– 20 January	Dark grey, black, dark brown Lead Turquoise, amethyst	Ivy, hemlock, medlar, heartease	Pine, elm, yew Hemp, comfrey, knap-weed
Aquarius *(Water carrier)* 21 January– 18 February	Turquoise or grey Aluminium Aquamarine	Orchid, laburnum	Fruit trees in general Herbs and species with sharp or unusual flavour
Pisces (Fish) 19 February– 20 March	Soft sea-green or blue Platinum or tin Moonstone or bloodstone	Water-lily	Willow, fig, trees that grow near water Saccharum, succory, lime flowers, mosses

APPENDIX

BOOKS

Any book list must be influenced by personal preferences, but this short selection will give readers the maximum information on various aspects of flower arranging.

Abstract and free-style
Design with plant material. Marian Aaronson, Grower Books, 1972.
Flower arrangement – free-style. Edith Brack, Whitethorn Press, 1977.
Flowers in the modern manner. Marian Aaronson, Grower Books, 1981.
Modern flower arranging. Edith Brack, Batsford 1982.
Scultura Floreale. Paola Burger & Loli Marsano, Idea Books Edizioni, Milan, 1986. (In Italian with English translation.)

Artificial flowers
Handmade flowers. Vera Jeffery & Malcolm Lewis, Hamlyn, 1980.

Bible plants
Bible plants at Kew. F N Hepper, HMSO, London, 1981.

Church flowers
Church flowers, month by month. Jean Taylor, Mowbray, 1979.
Flower decoration in churches. Sheila Macqueen, Faber, 1964. (Out of print.)
Flowers in church. Jean Taylor, Mowbray, 1976.

Colour
A flower arranger's guide to colour theory, NAFAS, 1971. (An inexpensive leaflet.)

Drying and preserving
The dried flower book. Mierhof & Boer Vlamings, Herbert Press, 1981.
Flowers that last. Pauline Mann, Batsford, 1984.
Making pressed flower pictures. Scott & Beazley, Batsford, 1979.
NAFAS arranging everlasting flowers. Compiled, Mary Newnes, Ebury Press, 1987.

Floristry
The Constance Spry Handbook of Floristry. Harold Piercy, Croom Helm, 1984.

General flower arrangement
The complete guide to flower and foliage arrangement. Iris Webb, Webb & Bower, 1979.
Creative flower arrangement. Jean Taylor, Stanley Paul, 1973.
Flower arranger's bible. Derek Bridges, Century, 1985.
Flower arranging. Daphne Vagg, Ward Lock, 1980.
Flower Decoration. George Smith, Webb & Bower, 1988.
Practical flower arranging. Jean Taylor (Hamlyn 1973).
The W. I. creative guide to arranging flowers. Edith Brack, W I Books, 1988.

History
European flower painters. Peter Mitchell, A & C Black, 1973.
Guide to period flower arranging. NAFAS, 1982.
A history of flower arrangement. Julia S. Berrall, Thames & Hudson, 1953.
The history of flower arranging. Edited Cooke & McNicol, Heinemann, 1989.

Houseplants
The gold-plated houseplant expert. D G Hessayon, pbi Publications and Century Hutchinson, 1987.

Ikebana
Ikebana. Takashi Sawano, Ward Lock, 1981.
Ikebana – a practical and philosophical guide. Stella Coe. Edited by Mary Stewart, Century 1984.

Plant names
Reader's Digest encyclopaedia of garden plants and flowers, Reader's Digest, 1971.
RHS Gardeners' Encyclopedia of plants and flowers. Ed. Christopher Brickell, Dorling Kindersley, 1989.

Shakespeare's plants
The world of Shakespeare: plants. Alan Dent, Osprey, 1971.

Shows and judging
Encyclopaedia of judging and exhibiting. Esther Veramae Hame'l, Ponderosa Publications, America, 1966.
Flower arranging for shows. Mary Napper, Batsford, 1984.

NAFAS publications
NAFAS guide to colour theory
NAFAS judges' manual
NAFAS handbook of schedule definitions
NAFAS show guide
NAFAS leaflet No. 7 – show work for beginners
European Continental Styles

Table decorations
Flowers for the table. Daphne Vagg, Batsford, 1983.

Weddings
Flowers for celebrations. Derek Bridges, Ebury Press, 1988.
Flowers for special occasions. Pulbrook & Gould, Batsford, 1982.
Wedding flowers. Pauline Mann, Batsford, 1985.
Flowers for weddings. Pamela McNicol, Batsford, 1991.

MAGAZINES

The two British flower arrangement magazines are:

Flora
A4-size page. Published six times a year. Available on bookstalls or by postal subscription to:
Flora, 77 Bulbridge Road, Wilton, Salisbury, Wilts SP2 OLE

The Flower Arranger
A5-size page. Published quarterly, it is the **NAFAS** (q.v.) magazine. Available from flower clubs or by annual postal subscription to the printers, Taylor-Bloxham, Nugent Street, Leicester, LE3 5HH

ADDRESSES

City & Guilds of London Institute, 76 Portland Place, London, WIN 4AA.
Flora. Postal subscriptions to: c/o The Riverside Press, 2–3 Grant Close, Gillingham Industrial Park, Gillingham, Kent, ME8 OPS. Editorial: Maureen Foster, 77 Bulbridge Road, Wilton, Salisbury, Wiltshire, SP2 OLE.
Flower Arranger, The. Individual subscriptions to: Taylor-Bloxham, Nugent Street, Leicester LE3 5HH. flower club members order through their club. Editor: Jill Grayston, Little Lions Farm, Ashley Heath, Ringwood, Hants, BH24 2EX.
Ikebana International Headquarters. CPO Box 1262, Tokyo, Japan.
Interflora. Interflora House, Sleaford, Lincolnshire, NG34 7TB.
NAFAS. National Association of Flower Arrangement Societies of Great Britain, 21 Denbigh Street, London, SWIV 2HF.
NAFAS Teachers Association. As above.
NCCPG. National Council for the Conservation of Plants and Gardens, c/o RHS Garden, Wisley, near Woking, Surrey, GU23 6QB.
RHS. Royal Horticultural Society, Vincent Square, London, SWIP 2PE.
RSNC. Royal Society for Nature Conservation, The Green, Nettleham, Lincoln, LN2 2NR.
Videos. See page 178:
Master Class series, Holiday Brothers Ltd, 172 Finney Lane, Heald Green, Cheadle Hulme, Cheshire, SK8 3PU.
Gerard Holdsworth Productions, 31 Palace Street, London, SWIE 5HW.
WAFA. Address obtainable from NAFAS, above.